Helion & Company Limited
Unit 8 Amherst Business Centre
Budbrooke Road
Warwick
CV34 5WE
England
Tel. 01926 499 619
Email: info@helion.co.uk
Website: www.helion.co.uk
Twitter: @helionbooks
https://helionbooks.wordpress.com/

Published by Helion & Company 2026
Text © Dewald Venter 2026
Colour profiles drawn by and © David Bocquelet 2026
Map drawn by b.b.h.illustrations © Helion & Company 2026

Cover: Ratel ZT3-A2. (C. Hugo)

Designed and typeset by Mach 3 Solutions (www.mach3solutions.co.uk)
Cover design Paul Hewitt, Battlefield Design (www.battlefield-design.co.uk)

ISBN: 978-1-804519-92-9

British Library Cataloguing-in-Publication Data
A catalogue record for this book is available from the British Library

Contents

Dedication   2
Abbreviations and Acronyms   2
Author's Note   3
Acknowledgements   3
Foreword   4
Introduction: Framing South African Armour Development   4

1   Eland Armoured Car   5
2   Buffel Mine-Protected Vehicle   14
3   Ratel Infantry Combat Vehicle   23
4   Casspir Mine-Protected Vehicle   36
5   G6 Rhino Self-Propelled Howitzer Vehicle   45
6   Ystervark   55
7   Bateleur Multiple Rocket Launcher   59
8   Olifant Mk1A Main Battle Tank   64

Bibliography   70
About the Author   72

Dedication

This book is dedicated to my father Carel Venter and mother Maryna Venter.

Abbreviations and Acronyms

2IC	Second in Command
61 Mech	61 Mechanised Battalion Group
32 Bn	32 Battalion
AAD	African Aerospace and Defence
AC	armoured car
AML	*Auto Mitrailleuse Légère* (Light Armoured Car)
AP	armour piercing
APC	armoured personnel carrier
APCT	armour-piercing core tracer
APDS	armour-piercing discarding sabot
APFSDS	armour-piercing fin-stabilised discarding sabot
APFSDS-T	armour-piercing fin-stabilised discarding sabot-tracer
APU	auxiliary power unit
ARMSCOR	Armaments Corporation of South Africa
ARV	armoured recovery vehicle
ATES	Artillery Target Engagement System
AU	African Union
BAE	British Aerospace
BMG	Browning Machine Gun
COIN	counterinsurgency
CSIR	Council for Scientific and Industrial Research
DENEL	South African armaments development and manufacturing company
DRU	Defence Research Unit
EBR	Panhard *Engin Blindé de Reconnaissance* (Armoured Reconnaissance Vehicle)
EAOS	Enhanced Observation and Surveillance
ER	extended range
ERFB	extended range full bore
ERFB-BB	extended range full bore-base bleed
ESD	Electronics System Development
EW	electronic warfare
FAPLA	People's Armed Forces of Liberation of Angola
ft	feet
ft/s	feet per second
FCS	fire control system
gal	gallon (US)
GPS	Global Positioning System
HE	high explosive
HE-I	high explosive incendiary
HEAT	high explosive anti-tank
HEAT-T	high explosive anti-tank tracer
HE-BB	high explosive base bleed
HE-FRAG	high explosive fragmentation
HESH	high explosive squash head
hp	horsepower
hp/t	horsepower per ton
HQ	headquarters
ICV	infantry combat vehicle
in	inch
IR	infrared
km	kilometre
km/h	kilometres per hour
lbs	pounds
LEW	Lyttelton Engineering Works
LMS	Launcher Management System
MBT	main battle tank
MCS	Modular Charge System
MECHEM	MECHanical and CHEMical Research
Mi	mile
Mk	mark
Mph	miles per hour
MPLA	Popular Movement for the Liberation of Angola
MRAP	mine-resistant ambush protected
MLRS	multiple launch rocket system
MRL	multiple rocket launcher
ms	millisecond
m/s	metres per second
MV MM DS	Mechem Vehicle Mounted Metal Detection System
NATO	North Atlantic Treaty Organization
NBC	Nuclear, Biological, Chemical
OMC	Olifant Manufacturing Company
QF	Quick Firing
RHA	rolled homogenous armour
RPG	rocket propelled grenade
SAAC	South African Armoured Corps
SAAF	South African Air Force
SADC	Southern African Development Community
SADF	South African Defence Force
SAHV	South African High-Velocity Missile
SAI	South African Infantry
SAMIL	South African Military
SANDF	South African National Defence Force
SAP	South African Police
SAPS	South African Police Service
SATNAV	satellite navigation
SATSC	South African Technical Service Corps
sec	seconds
SLEP	service life extension plan
SPAAG	self-propelled anti-aircraft gun
SPAAM	self-propelled anti-aircraft missile
SSB	Special Service Battalion
SWA	South West Africa
SWAPO	South West Africa People's Organisation
SWATF	South West Africa Territorial Force
t	ton
UCDD	United Car and Diesel Distributors
UN	United Nations
UNITA	National Union for the Total Independence of Angola
USSR	Union of Soviet Socialist Republics
VHF	very high frequency
V-LAP	Velocity-Enhanced Long-range Artillery Projectile
WP-SMK	white phosphorus smoke
WW2	World War Two
yd	yard

Author's Note

Writing a military book has been a lifelong dream and passion, one that continues to drive my academic research into military heritage. This updated edition, split into two volumes due to the size builds on the foundation of the first, with added depth and new revelations that enhance the narrative and celebrate South Africa's contributions to armoured vehicle development. The second edition now includes detailed histories of the Ystervark (Vol 1) and Bosvark (Vol 2), as well as an expanded account of the Rooikat's development (Vol 2). Additionally, prototype vehicles and new vehicle data have been incorporated, alongside a host of corrections and refinements to ensure the accuracy of the information presented.

The process of sourcing new data for this edition presented its own challenges. Given the comprehensive nature of the first edition, uncovering fresh insights required deep-dive archive searches, which fortunately uncovered some intriguing new information. I am also indebted to Reinhardt Ackerman, a fellow military vehicle enthusiast, whose meticulous work in uncovering archival promotional documents proved invaluable.

Perhaps the most significant personal revelation during the writing of this edition was the clarity I gained about the development history of the Olifant tank family. Understanding the why behind certain decisions and how those decisions influenced future developments has allowed me to provide a richer and more accurate account of this iconic vehicle.

Nearly every chapter in this edition has undergone some revision whether through the addition of new information, corrections to previous details, or expansions based on new sources made available to the public. While some chapters have undergone more substantial changes than others, the overall book reflects the most up-to-date and accurate information available at the time of writing.

The success of the first edition, with positive reviews from numerous formal reviewers and a 4.7 out of 5-star rating on Amazon from 55 reviewers, was immensely encouraging. It is my hope that this second edition will continue to serve as a definitive resource for anyone with an interest in South African armoured vehicles, military history, and the stories of the men and women who designed and operated these incredible machines.

Dewald Venter

Acknowledgements

This book represents the second edition, and over the four years it took to complete, I had the assistance of many individuals who designed, managed, tested, and used the vehicles featured within. Their firsthand knowledge and dedication helped transform ideas on paper into some of the finest military vehicles ever produced. Interviewing each of them gave me invaluable insight into the unique stories of these vehicles.

I would like to express my deepest gratitude to Brigadier General (retd) Tony Savides, one of the fathers of the Ratel and former SA Army project director who oversaw the design and production of several vehicles featured in this book. His willingness to assist, clarify, and point me in the right direction was invaluable. Together with several other key authors, Tony is finalising a two-volume book on the Ratel ICV, which I am sure will be a winner and an exciting read.

I also extend my thanks to Brigadier General (retd) André Retief, former General Officer Commanding SA Army Armour Formation. His support during his time as the GOC made research possible at the SA Army School of Armour, 1 SSB, and the SA Armour Museum.

Desmond Gardner, former Director of OMC Engineering, provided technical guidance and support throughout the process, always ready to lend a hand when needed.

To every interviewee I met in person, over the phone, via email, or social media, thank you for sharing your stories and perspectives.

A special thanks to the photo contributors for sharing their memories, which add depth to the text and enhance the book's visual impact. Also, my appreciation to the soldiers who shared their stories, diving deep into their experiences.

David Bocquelet, chief editor at Tank Encyclopaedia, deserves recognition for allowing me to join his team, and Stan Lucian for his tireless 11th-hour proofreading.

Andy Miles and Tom Cooper and the team from the @War Series have my gratitude for their enthusiasm in publishing my work.

To my wife, Carina, thank you for your support, encouragement, and understanding of my passion for writing military matters. To my daughter, Ciska, who is now in high school, thank you for your support and understanding for the times I had to step away and my parents for their unwavering support.

Lastly, to the next generation of authors, I hope this book inspires your imagination and love for military heritage. I encourage you to visit and support your local military museums.

Foreword

South African armoured Vehicles are somewhat unique in the way they were designed, developed and manufactured under most adverse conditions of isolation, sanctions and conflict, both domestic and external.

What ARMSCOR, and the South African industry at large, managed to achieve over several decades, post WW2, is truly remarkable. With creativity and ingenuity, born out of desperation, they forged ahead and purchased, modified, adapted and provided weapon systems against severe deadlines and under the adverse conditions mentioned.

The political, economic and military history of Southern Africa amply illustrates the remarkable success of these weapon systems and their role in shaping strategic and tactical outcomes.

Prof Venter has once again proved his acute understanding of, and passion for, these weapon systems that he studied and researched over several decades.

What a pleasure and privilege for me to be involved in a minor way with Venter's passion, and to provide a foreword to this excellently researched volume. Having served in and with most of these systems and having been involved in their development, deployment and eventual preservation in museums, I am only too pleased to enjoy the fruits of his labours.

This book is a "must have" reference for any armoured vehicle enthusiast and certainly provides an authentic reference document on all the South African armoured vehicles used post WW2.

André Retief, Brigadier General (retd)
Pretoria, Jan 25

Introduction: Framing South African Armour Development

A battlespace encompasses the environment, conditions, and circumstances within an operational area that influence both friendly and enemy military forces' (land, air, sea) ability to achieve their mission objectives. Key factors include terrain, infrastructure, weather, civilian presence, and available intelligence. The Southern African battlespace, like any, presents its own set of distinct challenges.

The African battlespace is characterised by its difficult terrain and environmental obstacles. These challenges include poor road infrastructure, limited access routes, vast distances to cover, dense and rugged terrain, and scarce resources for sustainment. Such conditions make movement, combat operations, and logistical support extremely challenging. Furthermore, de Vries notes that there were often multiple avenues of approach available, with expansive open spaces that allowed infiltration, and abundant cover for concealment from both ground and air detection.

The South African Defence Force (SADF) preferred wheeled vehicles over tracked ones for several reasons. In the Southern African battlespace, wheeled vehicles offered significant logistical and strategic advantages, including greater flexibility for rapid operations. Wheeled vehicles were 40–60% cheaper, had service lives up to 300% longer, and used 60% less fuel than tracked vehicles, with extended maintenance intervals ranging between 200–300%. Furthermore, wheeled vehicles required smaller power packs to achieve comparable performance to tracked ones. Tracked vehicles, being more vulnerable to landmine explosions, were often immobilised. In contrast, wheeled platforms like the Rooikat and Ratel could maintain mobility after a mine blast. The use of wheels, rather than tracks, provided better operational mobility over long distances and supported the manoeuvre warfare tactics employed by the SADF. This contrasted with the positional warfare approach of People's Armed Forces of Liberation of Angola (FAPLA) and Cuban forces.

South African vehicles were specifically designed and reinforced to withstand these harsh conditions, a capability referred to as *"bundu bashing"*. This term, which will be used throughout the book, describes the process of driving directly through small trees and dense vegetation rather than navigating around them. The ability of South African armoured vehicles to "break the bush" became a critical advantage, allowing them to avoid landmine-laden dirt roads and use indirect routes through dense vegetation. This tactic often caught FAPLA and Cuban forces by surprise, enabling the SADF to outmanoeuvre them and achieve their objectives.

Looking ahead, the future of armoured warfare in Southern Africa will likely be shaped by evolving geopolitical dynamics, technological advancements, and changing military doctrines. As regional threats become more complex and multifaceted, the role of armoured vehicles in both conventional and asymmetrical warfare will continue to be pivotal. Southern Africa's challenging terrain and vast landscapes will ensure that armoured vehicles remain indispensable for manoeuvre operations, counterinsurgency (COIN) efforts, and peacekeeping missions. However, with the increasing prevalence of unmanned systems and advanced robotics, there may be a shift toward more autonomous and digitally integrated platforms, enhancing the effectiveness of armoured units while reducing the risk to human soldiers.

The proliferation of advanced weaponry, such as precision-guided munitions and anti-tank systems, as well as cheap drones will further influence the design and operational use of armoured vehicles. Future Southern African armoured platforms may incorporate enhanced protection mechanisms, including Active Protection System and greater adaptability to emerging threats. As regional conflicts become more unpredictable, the continued development of armoured warfare strategies that focus on rapid deployment, versatility, and resilience will be essential for maintaining operational superiority.

1

Eland Armoured Car

The Eland armoured car (AC), affectionately nicknamed Noddy Car due to its small size and versatility, holds a special place in South African military history. Named after the African Eland, the largest antelope, the vehicle was designed to adapt to Southern Africa's demanding terrain. This chapter explores the Eland's development, its unique design features, and its operational legacy.

Development

In the late 1950s, South Africa's military, then known as the Union Defence Force, relied heavily on the Ferret AC. However, by the early 1960s, it became apparent that the Ferret would not meet the evolving military requirements of South Africa, which were increasingly shaped by the likelihood of expeditionary missions and counterinsurgencies. Recognising this shortcoming, the SADF sought to acquire a new, modern reconnaissance vehicle that was lightweight, lightly armoured, well-armed, and capable of operating over long ranges in Southern Africa's challenging terrain.

Initially, three ACs were considered: the Saladin, Panhard EBR, and Panhard AML. Ultimately, the Panhard AML was selected due to its adaptability and potential for local production. This decision marked the beginning of one of South Africa's most ambitious weapons manufacturing programmes: the development of the Eland AC.

The first trials of the AML 60, which was equipped with a 60mm Brandt Mle CM 60A1 breech-loading mortar, revealed that the vehicle lacked sufficient firepower. In response, South Africa requested a more powerful armament, prompting Panhard to design a new turret to accommodate the DEFA 90mm low-pressure quick firing (QF) gun. South Africa initially purchased 100 AMLs along with additional turrets, engines, and parts for the local assembly of 800 more ACs. The subsequent production of the AML 60 and AML 90 (rebranded the Eland 60 and Eland 90) became one of the most extensive arms manufacturing initiatives in post-Second World War South Africa.

Production by the South African industrial firm Sandock-Austral began in 1961, and the first batch of vehicles entered service trials in 1962 as the Eland Mk1. At this stage, the Eland was essentially still a French AML with 40% local content, as most parts were sourced from Panhard. In 1964, South Africa acquired the licence to independently manufacture the vehicle's hull and turret. The turret was produced

Eland 60 and Eland 90 leaving Etale Base in April 1978. (Open source)

by Austral Engineering in Wadeville, and the hulls were built by Sandock-Austral at their plants in Boksburg and Durban.

A series of continuous improvements followed to better suit the vehicle for African conditions. The Eland Mk2 featured improved steering and brakes, with 56 units delivered. The Eland Mk3 saw the addition of a custom-built fuel system, while the Eland Mk4 replaced the electric clutch with a more reliable conventional model and relocated the fire control system (FCS) from the gunner's feet to the turret hand crank. Minor enhancements, such as replacing the chain securing the fuel cap with a quieter cable, were also made. By 1967, 66% of the parts in South African-produced Elands were locally sourced, with only the exterior retaining its resemblance to the French AML.

From 1972 onwards, 356 Eland Mk5 vehicles were built, featuring a new General Motors 2.5ℓ water-cooled, four-cylinder inline petrol engine mounted on rails for easier field replacement reducing engine change time to just 40 minutes. The Eland Mk5 also introduced improved communication equipment, spring shock absorbers, and run-flat tyres for better operational efficiency.

The Eland Mk6 upgrade, introduced in 1975, brought 1,016 previously produced Eland vehicles up to the Mk5 standard. The final version of the vehicle, the Eland Mk7, was produced in 1979. It featured a raised commander's cupola derived from the Ratel infantry combat vehicle (ICV), repositioned headlamps from the lower glacis to a raised level, new power brakes, an improved transmission, and a lengthened frontal section to provide more comfort for taller South African soldiers.

The Eland 60 and Eland 90 became the standard ACs for the SADF's AC regiments. They served primarily in a reconnaissance role but were also integrated into tank regiments. The SADF deployed Elands with permanent forces at the SA Army School of Armour, 1 South African Tank Regiment, and 2 South African Tank Regiment. Among the reserve forces, the Eland was used by units such as the Natal Mounted Rifles, Umvoti Mounted Rifles, and Regiment Oranje Rivier, among others. In South West Africa (SWA), the Eland was deployed by South West Territorial forces and 2 South African Infantry (SAI) based in Walvis Bay.

The Eland was gradually phased out of frontline service in the late 1980s with the introduction of its indigenous successor, the Rooikat 76 AC, and was officially retired from South African National Defence Force (SANDF) service in 1994. Many Elands remain as gate guards at military bases, and several operational models are preserved in museums, including the South African Armour Museum in Bloemfontein. Some Elands have also entered private collections and foreign military museums.

By the end of its production, more than 1,600 Eland vehicles had been built. The Eland family, which also includes a version equipped with a 20mm QF cannon, continues to serve in the armed forces of several countries, including Benin, Burkina Faso, Chad, Gabon, Ivory Coast, Malawi, Morocco, Sahrawi Arab Democratic Republic, Senegal, Uganda, and Zimbabwe.

Design Features

The design of the Eland evolved significantly over time, allowing it to meet the challenges of Africa's diverse and demanding terrain. As a lightweight, yet heavily armed reconnaissance vehicle, the Eland combined mobility, firepower, and protection to create a versatile combat platform. The Eland's effectiveness on the battlefield stemmed from its design innovations. The following sections explore the key components of the Eland Mk7 namely its design, focusing on mobility, armament, and protection.

Mobility

Although not amphibious, the Eland could ford 82cm (32in) of water with the installation of plugs in the floor. It was powered by a General Motors four-cylinder, 2.5ℓ petrol engine capable of producing 87hp (65kW) at 4,600rpm. This provided a power-to-weight ratio of 16.4hp/t for the Eland 60 and 14.5hp/t for the Eland 90. The maximum road speed was 90km/h (56mph), with a recommended cruising speed of 80km/h (50mph). Over rough terrain, it could achieve 30km/h (18.6mph).

The Eland could cross a 0.5m wide ditch and ascend a 51% gradient. Equipped with two ditch-crossing channels on the front, the vehicle could traverse ditches up to 3.2m (10.5ft) wide using four

Eland 90. Exercise Thunder Chariot 1984. (J. Van Zyl photo collection)

Eland 60. (Open source)

Eland 90 driver's station. (S. Tegner)

channels. It had rack-and-pinion assisted power steering, which significantly improved the driver's handling of the vehicle in rough conditions. However, its ground clearance 380mm (15in) for the Eland 90 and 400mm (15.8in) for the Eland 60 combined with its four-wheel configuration, sometimes led to the vehicle becoming stuck during off-road travel.

Endurance and logistics

The Eland had a fuel capacity of 142ℓ (37.5gal), allowing it to cover 450km (280mi) on-road, 240km (149mi) off-road, and 120km (74.5mi) over-sand. The Eland 90 and 60 were both equipped with two 7.62mm machine guns, one co-axially mounted and the other positioned above the turret for close defence. The Eland 90 carried 3,800 rounds of machine gun ammunition, while the Eland 60 carried 2,400 rounds. With creative stacking, more ammunition could be stored.

At the rear of the turret, the vehicle housed B-56 long-range and B-26 short-range radios, which provided reliable tactical communication and enhanced command and control on the battlefield. This, combined with well-trained crews, allowed for coordinated assaults on enemy tanks like the T-54/55 during Operation Askari.

In the Mk7 version, a storage bin was added at the rear of the turret, which became essential for crew efficiency. Earlier versions did not have a built-in drinking water tank, requiring crews to carry water in a 20ℓ (5.2gal) jerry can mounted outside the driver's door. Crews improvised by storing non-drinking water in empty ammunition boxes and used gun casings mounted externally. The Mk7 model included a 40ℓ (10.5gal) drinking water tank installed at the rear, with access through a brass push tap.

Vehicle layout

The Eland carries a standard complement of three crew members: the commander, gunner, and driver. The commander's station is located on the left side of the turret, while the gunner is seated on the right. The turret is fitted with two L794D periscopes to allow for observation while the turret is closed. Additionally, a raised vision cupola is mounted in the turret roof above the commander's position, providing the commander with a 360-degree view from inside the turret. This setup enables the commander to direct the gunner onto a target by using a line-of-sight targeting system. For aiming the main armament, the gunner utilises an M494 sighting scope, which offers x6 magnification to ensure accurate firing.

Eland 90 gunner's station. Gun breech block (left), gunner's turret hand crank and firing switches (right), vertical aim drive (right of breech block). (S. Tegner)

Eland 90 rear of turret. An additional six round first stage ammunition rack on the left (right side of turret). Similar to the AML 90 there is a six and four round first stage ammunition rack right side (left side of turret) which is the same as on an AML 90. The radio equipment was located at the back of the turret, in-between the ammunition racks. (S. Tegner)

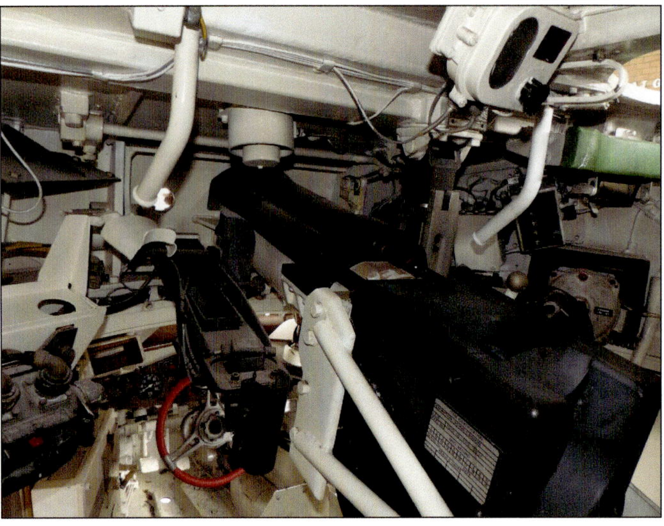

Eland 90 Commander`s station. Looking inwards towards the gun breech block (centre), gunner's turret hand crank and firing switches (right), commander's coaxial BMG (left of breech block). Notice commander's position (left) is slightly elevated compared to gunner's position (right). Gunner (right) has no cupola while commander (left) does. The layout is the same in the Ratel 90. (S. Tegner)

Rear view of Eland 90. (S. Tegner)

Eland 90 Mk7 Commanders vision cupola (right) and gunners hatch (left). (S. Tegner)

Entry and exit for both the commander and the gunner in the Eland 90 are through single-piece hatches, with one hatch for each position, both of which open to the rear. In the Eland 60, however, both the commander and gunner share an elongated hatch, which also opens to the rear. In emergency situations, both the commander and the gunner can escape through the driver's entry doors located on either side of the hull, between the forward or rear wheels. An additional feature of interest is the pistol port situated on the front left side of the hull, allowing the commander to fire a personal weapon from inside the vehicle, if necessary.

The driver's station is positioned at the front-centre of the hull and is accessible either through the side entry doors mentioned above or via a single-piece hatch that opens to the right above the driver's station. The driver's station provides limited adjustability, which can make it challenging for taller drivers to operate comfortably. The single-piece hatch at the driver's position contains three integrated periscopes, which enhance the driver's vision and situational awareness. For night operations, the central periscope can be replaced with a passive night-driving episcope, manufactured by Eloptro, allowing the vehicle to be operated in both day and night conditions.

Main armament

The Eland 90 was equipped with a GIAT 90mm F1 gun, known locally in South Africa as the GT-2 and produced by Denel Land Systems. This low-velocity cannon provided the vehicle with the firepower required to engage a wide range of targets, from lightly armoured vehicles to fortified positions. The Eland 90 was capable of firing HE, HEAT-T, WP-SMK, and canister rounds, making it a highly versatile asset during the South African Border War.

The HE round was effective at distances of up to 2.2km (1.36mi), while the HEAT-T round could engage targets at 1.2km (0.75mi) and was capable of penetrating up to 320mm (12.6in) of rolled homogenous armour (RHA) at zero degrees, or 150mm (5.9in) at a 60-degree angle. The HEAT-T round proved devastating against the T-34/85 tanks encountered by the South Africans in the early stages of the South African Border War. When more advanced tanks such as the T-54/55 entered the conflict, Eland 90 crews had to leverage their vehicle's small size and speed to flank the heavier tanks. It often took multiple shots from the Eland 90 to disable or destroy these newer tanks.

The HE round weighed 5.27kg (11.6lbs) and was highly effective against lightly armoured vehicles, enemy trenches, and bunkers. The Eland 90's recoil system used a single-cylinder with a permanent stress spring and a hydro-pneumatic recuperator to return the main gun to its original position after firing. A well-trained crew could fire the main gun every 8–10 seconds, whether the vehicle was static or at a short halt. The turret could rotate a full 360 degrees in under 25 seconds, though standard practise limited rotation to 90 degrees left or right of centre. The main gun had an elevation range of -8 to +15 degrees. Due to its compact size, the Eland 90 carried 29 rounds of main gun ammunition, with 16 rounds stored at the rear of the turret, five rounds behind the commander's seat, five behind the gunner's seat, and three at the bottom right of the turret basket.

The Eland 60 retained the original AML 60 turret, featuring the South African-manufactured 60mm M2 breech-loading gun-mortar. This weapon could fire a 1.72kg (3.7lbs) bomb at 200m/s (656ft/s), with a direct-fire range of up to 300m (328yd) and an indirect fire range of 2km (1.24mi). The vehicle carried 56 bombs in total,

consisting of both standard bombs and illumination rounds. The main armament on the Eland 60 had a wider elevation range than the Eland 90, capable of elevating from -11 to +75 degrees, making it particularly effective in both direct and indirect fire roles. The rate of fire was 6–8 bombs per minute, making it an ideal weapon for counterinsurgency and convoy protection roles. The Eland 60 was primarily deployed in SWA, particularly in the northern operational areas, where its main gun proved devastatingly effective against infantry targets.

Fire control system

The gunner in the Eland 90 uses an Eloptro x6 day sight for targeting. The process of laying the main gun is carried out manually via a hand-crank system, with the gunner aiming through a telescopic sight that is mechanically linked to the main gun. Unlike more advanced armoured vehicles, the Eland 90's main gun lacked stabilisation due to the absence of a turret drive. This limitation meant that the gunner had to manually adjust the weapon's aim, which could be challenging during movement or when engaging fast-moving targets.

Operating the Eland 90 required highly skilled crews who were trained to work together seamlessly. The absence of stabilisation demanded precision and coordination between the commander and gunner to engage enemy targets as quickly and effectively as possible. The crew had to balance speed and accuracy, often firing from short halts and then withdrawing rapidly to minimise their exposure to return fire. This tactic required not only expertise but also an understanding of the vehicle's limitations and advantages on the battlefield.

Protection

The Eland's welded steel-plated hull offered essential protection against battlefield threats, with thicknesses ranging from 8–12mm (0.3–0.47in). This armour provided effective defence against rifle fire, grenades, and artillery fragments, which were common threats in the operational environments it faced. However, the Eland was vulnerable to larger calibre weapons exceeding 12.7mm, as its light armour was not designed to withstand hits from such heavy firepower. Despite this, the Eland's small size and exceptional mobility often enabled it to evade direct hits, increasing its chances of survival in hostile environments.

To further enhance its survivability, the Eland was equipped with two banks of electrically operated 81mm smoke grenade launchers, mounted on the rear left and right sides of the turret. These launchers were used for self-screening purposes, allowing the crew to deploy smoke and withdraw from dangerous situations. Interestingly, there are two tubes located behind the left smoke grenade launchers, often mistaken for part of the smoke system. These tubes, however, serve a different function: they are used to store the main gun-cleaning brush.

Additional protection measures included the frontal headlamps, which were mounted on the frontal glacis and covered with armour to prevent damage from obstacles like thick brush when driving off-road.

Due to its compact size, the Eland was not equipped with an integrated fire suppression system. However, the crew was provided with several hand-held fire extinguishers. One extinguisher was mounted on the front right exterior of the vehicle, above the right wheel, while another was located inside the crew compartment to allow for quick responses to fires that might occur during combat.

Eland Family

Eland 20

In 1971, the South African Armoured Corps (SAAC) requested an Eland variant fitted with a 20mm main gun. An Eland 60, named *Vuilbaard* (Dirty Beard), was fitted with a Hispano-Suiza 20mm as a feasibility test. However, the results were not satisfactory, prompting further development. In early 1972, the same vehicle was modified again, this time with an F2 20mm cannon (imported for the Ratel 20 ICV project) mounted in a new turret. Both the Hispano-Suiza and F2 turrets were tested in a shoot-off, and the F2 came out on top. By then, the SAAC dropped the requirement for a 20mm armed Eland, choosing instead to focus on the Eland 60 and Eland 90 variants.

Eland 20. Right side view. (Open source)

Eland 20. Left side view. (Open source)

The Eland 20 used the exact same turret as the Ratel 20 and was armed with the 20mm F2 cannon, capable of firing in single shot, single automatic (80r/m), and full automatic (750r/m) modes. An advantage of this design was its dual-feed, allowing the gunner to switch between HE and AP rounds with the flick of a switch. The Eland 20 retained the coaxial 7.62mm machine gun and could also mount an additional 7.62mm machine gun on the roof for close defence. Around 1980–1981, Morocco purchased 30 Eland 20 ACs, marking the vehicle's only notable foreign service.

Eland ENTAC

In the late 1960s, the SADF conducted a war game simulating an invasion of SWA. One of the major shortcomings identified was that the Eland 90 lacked the necessary firepower to engage enemy main battle tanks (MBTs). To address this issue, two external rails were added to the Eland turret, each capable of carrying an ENTAC wire-guided anti-tank missile. This modification was tested, but the project never progressed beyond the trial phase and did not enter service.

Eland 90TD

As the Eland 90 phased out of SADF service, Reumech OMC saw an opportunity to improve the Eland Mk7 for potential foreign sales. The Eland 90TD was equipped with a turbocharged, water-cooled four-cylinder diesel engine, which provided similar horsepower to the petrol engine of the Mk7 but was more reliable and significantly less flammable. Although it is unclear if any Eland 90TD variants were sold, the Mechanology Company also upgraded AML 90 vehicles for Mali, adding a diesel engine and day/night fighting capability to meet specific operational needs.

Operational History

The Eland served with distinction in the SADF for nearly three decades, the majority of which were spent during the South African Border War. As anticipated, the conflict primarily took the form of a cross-border insurgency, and the Eland was deployed to the northern part of SWA in 1969 to counter the threat posed by People's Liberation Army of Namibia (PLAN) insurgents. These insurgents soon began a campaign of mine warfare to disrupt South Africa's transportation and logistics network, a tactic that would continue for two decades. In response, Eland vehicles were tasked with escorting convoys, but it quickly became apparent that their off-road mobility was limited, and they were highly vulnerable to landmines.

This vulnerability led to the development of more robust, mine-resistant vehicles such as the Buffel and Casspir MPV, which would take over the patrolling and counterinsurgency roles. Out of necessity, South Africa became a world leader in the development of mine-resistant vehicles, a direct result of the challenges faced during the South African Border War.

Despite these challenges, the Eland 90 played a valuable role as a reconnaissance, anti-armour, and fire support platform during the South African Border War. It participated in several key operations, including Savannah, Reindeer, Sceptic, Protea, and Askari. However, it was during Operation Askari that the limitations of the Eland 90 were fully realised. The introduction of T-54/55 MBTs by FAPLA stretched the Eland 90's capabilities to their limit, as the heavily armoured tanks required multiple hits from several ACs to disable or destroy them. The limited number of main gun rounds carried by the Eland, combined with the strain placed on the gun's recoil system, made such engagements increasingly problematic. Moreover, the Eland 90's off-road performance could not match that of the Ratel 90, further highlighting its shortcomings.

A review panel post-Operation Askari noted the advancing age of the Eland 90 as one of the primary shortcomings of the operation. As a result, the anti-armour role was passed to the Ratel 90, which utilised the same turrets as the Eland 90, but its height advantage allowed for better situational awareness, in addition to its superior overall performance. Consequently, the Eland 60 and 90 were relegated to tasks such as escorting convoys, conducting joint patrols, guarding strategic installations, manning roadblocks, and conducting search-and-destroy operations in SWA. Additionally, the Eland 90 was used as a training vehicle for Ratel 90 crews.

The final significant use of the Eland occurred during Operation Moduler, at the height of the South African Border War. On 5 October, Eland 90s, supported by infantry armed with anti-tank weaponry, set up an ambush north of Ongiva. The ambush was successful, as SADF forces destroyed a FAPLA motorised contingent, consisting of BTR-60s, BTR-40 APCs, and truck-mounted infantry, as they advanced toward Ongiva.

Conclusion

By the end of the South African Border War in 1989, the Eland's time in frontline service was coming to a close. Although it was replaced by the more advanced Rooikat, the Eland remained a symbol of South Africa's ability to innovate under pressure. Its successful service record across numerous campaigns, combined with its enduring legacy, ensures the Eland's lasting importance in South African military history. The vehicle's presence is still felt in museums and private collections, where it serves as a testament to South Africa's military ingenuity.

For a brief period, the SADF considered keeping at least one squadron of Elands in active service, anticipating the potential need for an air-portable armour capability. However, this plan was quickly set aside due to the remote possibility of deploying forces outside the border, as well as the ongoing pressure to reduce older equipment from service. Ultimately, the new SANDF retired the Eland from service in 1994.

In hindsight, this decision proved to be premature, as the SANDF would soon be involved in United Nations (UN) peacekeeping missions across Africa, where the demand for lightweight, mobile, and versatile armoured vehicles became evident. Despite this, the Eland remains in service with several African countries, continuing its legacy as a reliable and effective armoured vehicle across the continent.

Springbok MC-90: The MECHEM Concept Armoured Car

Following the end of the South African Border War, the SADF faced significant budgetary constraints. The post-war climate saw a scaling down of defence priorities, including the phasing out of several ageing systems, among them the Eland 90 armoured car. Strategists of the time argued against future expeditionary deployments beyond South Africa's borders, reducing the perceived need for air-transportable armour.

However, this position proved short sighted. South Africa's growing role in regional peacekeeping under the African Union (AU) would soon demand exactly such capabilities. A brief proposal to retain a squadron of Eland 90s for airborne use was considered but ultimately shelved. This decision left a critical gap in mobile, deployable firepower, one that would become increasingly evident during future deployments across the continent.

In this context, MECHEM, a specialised R&D division of ARMSCOR, was tasked with exploring practical alternatives using existing infrastructure and logistical stock. The idea was not to launch a full production programme, but to demonstrate what possible using in-service components, local expertise, was and operational feedback gathered directly from soldiers in the field.

MECHEM, which comprised vehicle, explosives, and weapons technology teams, had previously developed the Yster Arend (Iron Eagle) as part of Operation Jug a project to replace the ageing Ferret for airborne forces. Built on a Unimog chassis, the Iron Eagle was well received but later sold under licence to Alvis Vehicles in the UK, becoming the Acorn and later the Scarab.

Building on this experience, MECHEM constructed the Springbok prototype, officially designated MC-90 (M = MECHEM, C = Concept, 90 = calibre). The MC-90 mounted a 90mm gun turret onto a mine-protected Unimog-based hull. Developed in under a year, the concept vehicle showcased what could be achieved using off-the-shelf parts at a fraction of conventional costs. At the time, seven Springboks could be built for the cost of a single Rooikat 76. While not equal in combat power, its cost-efficiency and battlefield utility offered a compelling interim solution. Some suggest that its existence motivated the Rooikat development team to resolve teething issues more swiftly.

The Springbok was a 6-ton, 4×4 armoured car designed for air transportability and African terrain. Its mine-protected hull, coil spring suspension, and 125hp (93kW) diesel engine allowed it to traverse challenging off-road environments. The vehicle had a crew of three and was armed with a Denel GT-2 90mm low-velocity cannon, supported by two 7.62mm machine guns. It carried 29 main gun rounds and 3,800 rounds for the MGs.

The MC-90 featured basic optical sights and hand-cranked turret controls. While the gun was not stabilised, a trained crew could engage targets with relative efficiency. Its protection included 8–12mm steel plating, smoke grenade launchers, and fire suppression systems.

Though never adopted, the Springbok MC-90 stands as an example of practical innovation under constraint, a 'what-if' vehicle that highlighted South African ingenuity. The only prototype built was donated to the SA Armour Museum in Bloemfontein in 2014 and ceremonially named *Oom Frik* in honour of Honorary Colonel Frik Jankowitz's contributions to the museum and armoured heritage.

Springbok. SA Armour Museum. (D. Venter)

THE BATTLE OF BRIDGE 14 – THE ROLE OF THE ELAND

On the morning of 11 December 1975, the first light over Quibala revealed a tense, uneasy calm. Commandant Kruys had ordered the attack to begin at dawn, hoping to catch the enemy off guard. Battle Group Foxbat headquarters was relocated to a secure observation point from which the unfolding battle could be monitored without exposing personnel to unnecessary risk.

While Battle Group Foxbat took the frontline against FAPLA, Battle Group Bravo was tasked with protecting the western and rear approaches to Task Force Zulu's flank. The FAPLA company-level commanders Captains Anaya and Samoa deployed roughly a battalion of infantry, including Cuban troops, in depth, supported by anti-tank Sagger missiles positioned to threaten the advancing Eland armoured cars. Despite the threat, the terrain and deployment limited the Saggers' effectiveness. Behind the frontline, FAPLA's second defensive line included 120mm mortars, 76mm guns, 14.5mm anti-aircraft guns, and 122mm multiple rocket launchers, including at least one or maybe two mobile BM-21 multiple rocket launcher.

At 06:00, the artillery opened the battle with a massive preparatory bombardment, marking phase one. Major Blaauw, commanding Battle Group Foxbat's 140mm artillery, struck first at two 76mm guns at Kraaltjie (roughly 1km east of Bridge 14). Within moments, the enemy abandoned their positions, leaving guns and ammunition behind. Blaauw's next target was a 120mm mortar position at Almeida (800m due north of Bridge 14). The Cuban battery's vehicles and munitions were quickly destroyed, and inflicting heavy casualties.

A third target, another 120mm mortar battery 2km north of Almeida, was also neutralised after a few rounds. The enemy's batteries were inconsistently deployed, sometimes four, sometimes six guns, allowing Commandant Van der Westhuizen to bring the 140mm guns within effective range of the enemy's 122mm multiple rocket launchers. By 07:00, the artillery phase had achieved its objectives.

With the enemy's ammunition depots burning, Lieutenant Louw van Vuuren's lead troop advanced with four Eland 90 armoured cars accompanied by a company of UNITA (National Union for the Total Independence of Angola) soldiers under Captain Arto. The terrain ahead was marshy and difficult, but the Elands' mobility proved decisive.

Emerging from the lowlands, the armoured cars opened fire with their 90mm guns, striking one of the mortar pits, and the stored ammunition detonated in a violent chain of explosions, silencing the battery. This action removed the immediate threat and allowed the infantry to advance with minimal casualties. Behind the lead armoured cars, Captain Ferreira's Freedom Fighters seized Kraaltjie with little resistance. The enemy's

artillery remained, but the Elands' rapid manoeuvres and heavy firepower created confusion and prevented organised counterattacks. When enemy armoured cars appeared, Captain Fourie directed his Elands to occupy high ground, outflanking and overwhelming the opposition.

Lieutenant Jansen van Vuuren's Eland crew, after exhausting their main and coaxial ammunition, continued to fight using small arms through the gun ports, engaging enemy infantry at roughly 400 to 500 metres. When his own armoured car ran completely dry, Jansen van Vuuren, without hesitation, dismounted under fire and attacked the enemy with his pistol, reportedly killing several Cuban soldiers in close combat. His courage and determination in this action later earned him the Honoris Crux – an enduring testament to the fighting spirit of the Eland crews and their pivotal role at Bridge 14.

Battle Group Foxbat did not pause at Cassamba to consolidate but pressed on. At Bridge 15 (due north of Bridge 14), the enemy attempted to use anti-tank weapons to keep the Elands at bay. The second troop, under Lieutenant André Freyer, counterattacked, gradually reclaiming the field and driving enemy artillery crews from their positions. UNITA`s Captain Kanga Huchi captured Koppies despite being wounded, with Captain Ferreira's forces securing the area.

By the end of the battle, FAPLA had suffered approximately 250 casualties, while UNITA incurred only minor injuries. Battle Group Foxbat captured significant weapons, most importantly a BM-21 mobile multiple rocket launcher, further enhancing their combat capability. The Elands' presence throughout the engagement had been decisive, demonstrating the armoured car's versatility in both offensive manoeuvres and support roles.

The Eland 90 provided speed, firepower, and protection, enabling infantry to advance, disrupting enemy formations, and neutralising mortar positions before they could inflict significant damage. Even when rain turned the battlefield into a mud-choked quagmire, the armoured cars continued to perform critical tasks, including resupply runs and ambush clearing.

In retrospect, the Battle of Bridge 14 was a textbook example of combined arms tactics artillery preparation, armoured car manoeuvre, and coordinated infantry advances working in unison. The success of the operation ultimately hinged on the Elands' ability to deliver swift, accurate firepower, absorb enemy pressure, and create the conditions for infantry to achieve their objectives with minimal losses. At the same time, the artillery's role in neutralising key threats and enemy concentrations was decisive; without that support, the armoured cars would have been shredded by well-directed crossfire.

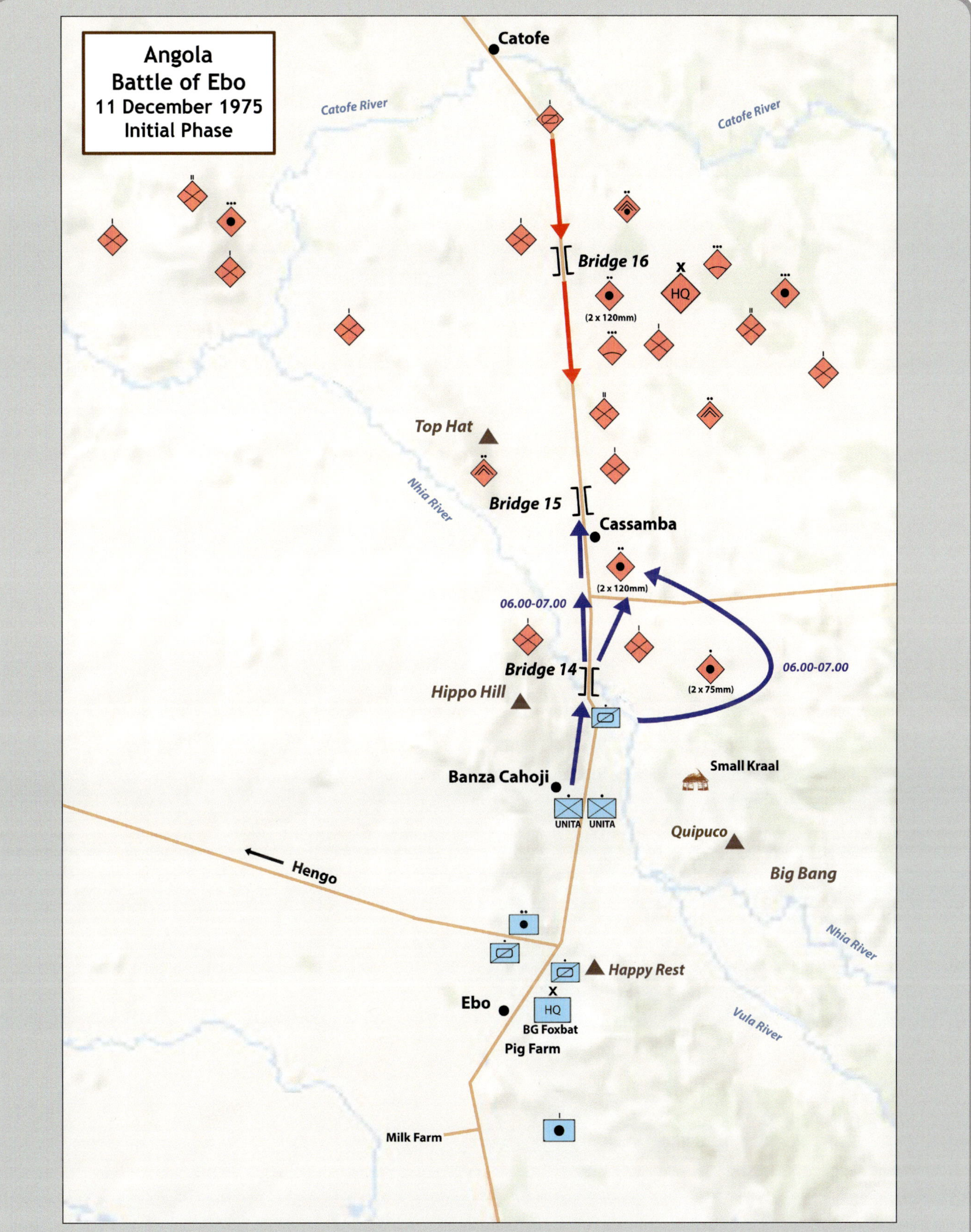

This is a reconstruction of the initial phase of the Battle of Ebo (also known as the Battle of the Bridge 14), on 11 December 1975. Precise details on the dispositions of the FAPLA units – 'corseted' by a contingent of advisors from the Cuban Military Mission in Angola (MMCA) – remain unavailable. Unlike other clashes in the same area, but further north-west, in November 1975, the Cuban documentation on the fighting around Bridge 14 between 8 and 12 December 1975 remains unavailable. Based on information about the situation from about two weeks earlier, it can be assessed that the combined FAPLA-MMCA force had a strength of two infantry battalions (each including three infantry companies), reinforced by batteries of ZPU-1 anti-aircraft machine guns, two teams with 120mm mortars, at least two 76mm ZiS-3 guns, several 9P132 Grad-P 122mm rocket launchers, and (according to South African accounts) one team operating Soviet-made 9M14 *Malyutka* (ASCC/NATO reporting name 'AT-3 Sagger') anti-tank guided missiles. Moreover, once the fighting began, a company of BRDM-2 armoured scout cars reached the scene by crossing Bridge 16 and attacking in a southern direction. (Map by b.b.h.illustrations)

2

Buffel Mine-Protected Vehicle

The Buffel MPV marked a revolutionary advancement in South Africa's military transport capabilities, following in the footsteps of the earlier Hippo MPV. As the first mass-produced mine-protected vehicle for the SADF, the Buffel quickly became a symbol of survival in one of the most hostile environments for infantry operations, SWA. Built with a focus on durability and safety, the Buffel was specifically designed to combat the growing threat of landmines, which were a significant risk during the South African Border War.

The Buffel's unique design allowed it to save countless lives by offering protection to soldiers in a high-risk combat zone, making it an essential asset in counterinsurgency operations. Its rugged construction and mine-resistant features allowed it to withstand the constant threat of landmines, improving the mobility of South African forces while safeguarding infantry units during operations.

The Buffel remained in active service throughout the 1980s, playing a crucial role in SADF operations, but was gradually phased out of frontline service by the end of that decade. It was eventually relegated to internal security duties and replaced by the more advanced Mamba APC in 1995. Despite its retirement, the Buffel's impact on mine-resistant vehicle development has had a lasting legacy, with its design paving the way for future armoured vehicles.

Development

By 1973, the threat posed by landmines in SWA had become a significant challenge for the SADF. South West Africa People's Organisation (SWAPO) insurgents frequently targeted South African patrols with anti-personnel and anti-tank landmines, which led to the urgent need for a dedicated mine-protected vehicle. Early attempts to modify existing vehicles, such as reinforcing Unimog trucks with sandbags, proved ineffective. This prompted the SADF to develop the Buffel, a purpose-built mine-protected vehicle designed to shield its occupants from explosive blasts while maintaining off-road mobility.

In the 1960s, the SADF purchased 200 Mercedes-Benz Unimog S (416.162) trucks, which featured a more powerful OM352 6-cylinder, water-cooled diesel engine. Due to the increasing threat of landmines, the Defence Research Unit (DRU) was tasked with improving the survivability of the Unimog fleet. The improvement to the Unimog chassis led to the development of the Bosvark vehicle, produced at 61 Base Workshop Unit in Pretoria.

The Bosvark featured a V-shaped rear tub made of mild steel, replacing the standard seat section, while the driver's cab received a Barber deflection plate to deflect mine detonation blasts. These modifications, while successful, did not protect the occupants from small arms fire. A total of 56 Bosvarks were produced and successfully used during Operation Savannah, the first major military incursion into Angola by the SADF in support of UNITA against the FAPLA and Cuban forces.

Following Operation Savannah, the SADF conducted a comprehensive review of their fleet, which led to the development of the SAMIL range of vehicles. During this time, Messrs UCDD

Buffel MPV. Exercise Thunder Chariot 1984. (J. Van Zyl photo collection)

(United Car and Diesel Distributors), the company that upgraded the Unimogs, heard of the Bosvark's development and sought to further evolve it into a dedicated MPV that could also function as an APC. Under the leadership of Koos de Wet, the Bosvark II took shape, incorporating several improvements.

A presentation was made to ARMSCOR in early 1976, and a wooden mock-up was completed by April 1976. This mock-up was presented to officials from the SADF, ARMSCOR, the Department of Trade and Industry, and the DRU. However, due to the planned phase-out of the Unimog in favour of the SAMIL vehicles, ARMSCOR's support for the Bosvark II waned. The development team relied on their own resources and support from the DRU to continue the project.

By August 1976, the final prototype of the Bosvark II was ready and underwent mobility and durability tests. These tests took place on a farm near Zeerust, where the Bosvark II was put through its paces by representatives from various interested groups. While some improvements were identified, the Bosvark II was certified as meeting the necessary standards. Nine more test vehicles were built and delivered to the SADF for further testing in the Northern Transvaal and Ovamboland. Following successful tests, a quotation was requested for more vehicles from UCDD.

In 1976, a live blast test was arranged with Koos de Wet in attendance to witness the test. Explosives were placed under the front left wheel of the vehicle, and in place of a human occupant, a drugged female baboon drafted into SADF service was strapped into the driver's seat. After a massive explosion, the vehicle's left wheel was blown off, but the baboon survived the blast and was treated for a small cut on its lip. The success of this test convinced the experts that the Buffel could protect its occupants from mine detonations. Subsequently, the SADF officially named the vehicle the Buffel and moved forward with its production.

Production of the Buffel began with 61 Base Workshop assisting in the disassembly of the SADF Unimog fleet, which was converted into Buffels. The first 19 Buffels were sent to Grootfontein in SWA in the latter half of 1977, and the first Buffels were deployed operationally in 1978. Over the next 17 years, 2,985 Buffels were produced.

The Buffel Mk1 retained the same Mercedes-Benz OM352 engine used in the Unimog and was fitted with a bush guard at the front to protect the vehicle from damage while driving through rough terrain. The Mk1A introduced an improvement with a drum brake system instead of the disc brakes used on the Mk1, and it was fitted with an Atlantis diesel engine (a licenced copy of the Mercedes-Benz engine). The Mk1B and subsequent variants used the same licenced engine and replaced the drum brakes with disc brakes. The Buffel Mk2 would have introduced a redesigned passenger tub, featuring all-round visibility through bulletproof windows, an armoured roof, and a rear entry and exit door, but this version was never implemented.

The Buffel served across nearly all branches of the SADF until its retirement in 1995. During its production phase, all chassis were produced and assembled in East London, while the armoured hulls were produced at Steelmobile Engineering in Rosslyn, Pretoria, and mounted onto the chassis. At its peak, the production rate increased to six vehicles per day with a single shift. In 1983, the price of a completed Buffel was R45,535, equivalent to R779,657 today.

The Buffel was used by various government sectors in SWA, including Water Affairs and the Roads Department. It was also used by Koevoet in the early 1980s before being replaced by the Casspir MPV. The only foreign country to purchase Buffels directly from the South African government was Sri Lanka, which acquired 185 vehicles. Other countries either bought Buffels through SADF auctions or the private sector. A handful of countries still use the Buffel (or its variants), including Malawi, Sri Lanka, Uganda, and Zambia.

Design Features

The Buffel was engineered with a single, crucial objective: to maximise crew survivability in the event of a landmine detonation. To achieve this, its design incorporated several critical elements. Most notably, the Buffel featured a high ground clearance and a

Buffel MPV at the War and Peace Revival 2019. (C. Moore)

Buffel MPV at the War and Peace Revival 2019. (C. Moore)

V-shaped hull, which deflected the force of explosions away from the crew compartment, significantly reducing the impact of blast damage. This V-shaped hull became a hallmark of mine-protected vehicles and was instrumental in protecting the Buffel's occupants from explosive blasts. Additionally, the upper structure was reinforced to minimise the risk of injury from shrapnel or debris. These combined features made the Buffel one of the most effective MPVs of its era.

The rugged African terrain, known for its harsh conditions, posed additional challenges that the Buffel was specifically designed to withstand. Its robust and simplified construction allowed for field repairs even after suffering significant damage from landmine detonations, although these repairs could still be costly. However, being a chassis-based MPV, the Buffel did not offer the same level of protection to its driveline as modern monocoque hull designs. Despite this limitation, the Buffel's simplicity and use of commercially available parts shortened its logistical chain, ensuring that most repairs could be carried out in the field without the need for specialised maintenance support.

Mobility

The Buffel was built on the Unimog 4×4 chassis, originally designed for difficult off-road conditions in Europe, making it well-suited for the challenging African battlespace. The vehicle's suspension system consisted of single-coil springs on the front axle and double-coil springs on the rear axle, which provided both stability and flexibility over rough terrain. The Buffel boasted a ground clearance of 420mm (16.54in) and could ford 1m (3.3ft) of water, making it highly capable in a variety of off-road environments.

However, its high ground clearance and narrow width made the vehicle somewhat top-heavy, which occasionally caused problems for inexperienced drivers. Turning too sharply at speed or driving on uneven or slippery terrain could lead to the vehicle rolling over. For passengers unaccustomed to the Buffel's swaying motion, especially on rough terrain, the passenger tub earned the nickname *kots koets* (vomit carriage).

The Buffel's engine produced 125hp (93kW) at 2,800rpm and was coupled to an eight-speed synchromesh manual transmission (eight forward and four reverse gears). Its transfer box was integrated with the gearbox, allowing for in-motion switching between 2×4 and 4×4 drive, which provided equal 50% power distribution between the front and rear axles. The vehicle was fitted with 12.50×20 wheels, which contributed to its off-road performance.

As an experimental measure, each wheel was filled with approximately 60ℓ (15.8gal) of water to help absorb the explosive force from landmines. However, this added around 300kg (661lbs) to the vehicle's overall weight, which negatively impacted its range and led to failures in the suspension, wheel bearings, and axle. Due to these issues, the water-filled wheel experiment was quickly discontinued.

Endurance and logistics

The Buffel was equipped with a 200ℓ (52.8gal) fuel tank, providing it with an impressive operational range of 1,000km (621mi) on-road and 500km (311mi) off-road. This extended range made the Buffel highly efficient for long missions in remote areas, reducing the need for frequent refuelling. The vehicle could reach a maximum road speed of 96km/h (60mph) and maintain 30km/h (19mph) in off-road conditions, allowing it to navigate diverse terrains effectively.

The Buffel's modular design facilitated easier maintenance and reduced logistical challenges, as damaged components could be quickly replaced. The use of commercially available parts further simplified repairs and lowered overall maintenance costs, ensuring the vehicle remained operational even in the harshest conditions.

Vehicle layout

The Buffel was composed of three primary components: the chassis, an armoured driver's cab positioned at the front left of the vehicle, and an armoured passenger tub located in the centre rear. The engine was mounted on the front right-hand side, with the transmission situated between the engine and the driver's cab. This arrangement allowed for the easy replacement of the engine and transmission in the event of damage from a mine detonation.

The driver's cab featured three rectangular bulletproof glass windows for visibility and was designed with an open top. The cab's base was wedge-shaped and secured to the chassis using cables, which helped mitigate the effects of blasts. Access to the cab was via a single door on the left side, along with two steel steps for easier entry. Later Buffel variants were equipped with a high-density polyethylene roof cover over the driver's cab for added protection. Inside the cab, the gear selection was located on the driver's right-hand side, and a spare wheel was mounted on the right side of the cab. Both the driver's and passengers' seats were blast resistant, designed to protect the spine in the event of a mine detonation. The Buffel retained its left-hand drive configuration due to the German origin of the chassis design.

Buffel MPV driver's station at the War and Peace Revival 2019. (C. Moore)

Buffel MPV driver's station at the War and Peace Revival 2019. (C. Moore)

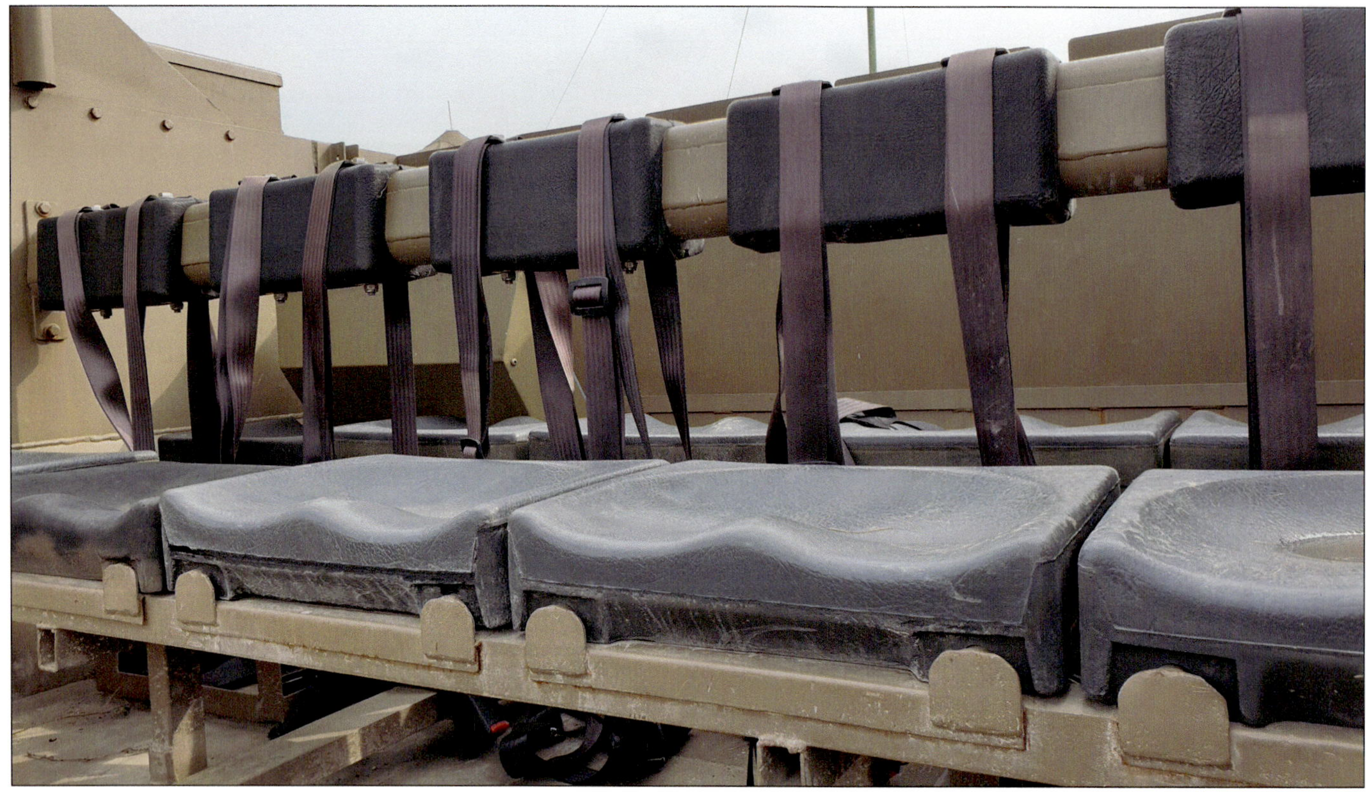

Buffel MPV passenger tub at the War and Peace Revival 2019. (C. Moore)

Access to the passenger tub was provided by two pairs of incremental steel steps on either side. Inside, the seating was arranged in two rows of five seats, facing outward from the centre. Each seat was equipped with harnesses to secure the occupants in case of a mine detonation or accidental rollover, which could otherwise result in passengers being ejected from the vehicle. An anti-roll bar was installed over the top of the passenger tub, preventing it from rolling over completely during a rollover incident. The left and right sides of the passenger tub contained horizontal panels with semi-circular grooves that allowed passengers to fire their rifles from their seats. During engagements, passengers would dismount by jumping over the side of the vehicle. Although the panels were horizontally hinged for ease of dismounting, they were rarely opened during movement, as they had a tendency to flip backward over rough terrain, potentially causing injury.

Traditionally, the section leader sat in the front left to facilitate communication with the driver. The Browning machine gun (BMG) team sat at the rear left alongside the 2IC, who operated the rear-facing machine gun. The number one rifleman sat in the front right, manning the front-facing machine gun, while the remainder of the section sat on the right side of the vehicle.

At the rear of the passenger tub was a large storage box made from high-density polyethylene. Passengers used the lower part of this storage box to store spare kit, while the upper section was designated for the driver's use. Occasionally, a road-killed warthog would be stored in the box for later consumption by the crew. The rear of the chassis also featured a water tap, which was connected to a 100ℓ (26.4gal) freshwater tank, providing a convenient water supply for the crew.

Protection

The Buffel was designed to protect its occupants from the most common threats encountered during operations, particularly landmine detonations. The vehicle could withstand the blast of a single TM-57 anti-tank mine equivalent to 6.34kg (14lbs) of TNT under the hull or a double TM-57 anti-tank mine equivalent to 12.6kg (27.7lbs) TNT under any of its wheels. The V-shaped armoured hull was critical in this protection, as it deflected the blast energy and fragments away from the driver and passenger tub, reducing the impact of explosions.

The driver's cab was fitted with bulletproof windows, ensuring the driver's safety from small arms fire. The plastic fuel and water tanks were strategically placed within the passenger tub's V-shaped hull, helping absorb blast energy from mine detonations, and further enhancing crew survivability. The armoured driver's cab and passenger tub protected against small arms fire, including 7.62×51mm NATO and 7.62×39mm AK-47 ball ammunition, as well as against explosive fragments, which were common in the combat environment.

Main armament

The Buffel's standard armament typically consisted of either a single or dual pintle-mounted 7.62mm BMG, positioned on the forward right-hand side of the passenger tub and/or the rear left-hand side. In some cases, twin mountings were observed, with the gunners receiving a gun shield for additional protection. These placements were effective in open terrain, allowing gunners to engage targets from multiple angles.

However, the forward-mounted armament often encountered difficulties when operating in thick bush. Branches could easily obstruct the gun's movement, reducing its effectiveness and making it difficult to maintain proper aim. Despite these challenges, the Buffel's armament provided adequate defensive capability during patrols and engagements.

The Buffel Family

The Buffel spawned several variants over the years to meet different operational needs, including a 2.5-ton Cargo Carrier and an Ambulance variant, both of which were adapted from the original Buffel design to serve logistical and medical roles in the field.

Moffel

During urban operations from 1991 to 1993 to quell increasing civil unrest and faction fighting in South Africa, a redesigned version of the Buffel, called the Moffel, was introduced to improve all-around safety. The original open driver's cab and passenger tub were enclosed to protect against petrol bombs and other dangerous projectiles. The horizontal drop-down panels on the passenger tub were replaced with bulletproof glass windows, each featuring two firing ports for self-defence. A rear access door with a bulletproof window was added to facilitate entry and exit, and a bulletproof window was also fitted on the forward right side of the vehicle.

The passenger tub redesign reduced its capacity from 10 to eight passengers, with the seating now facing inward. Hatches on the top of the tub allowed passengers to open them for additional visibility. These improvements significantly enhanced the vehicle's all-round vision and protection. However, the modifications increased the vehicle's weight by 800kg (1,764lbs), which strained the chassis, making it unsuitable for heavy off-road use. As a result, only a limited number of Moffel vehicles were produced, and they were restricted to road use.

Moffel MPV (front right). Sandstone Heritage Estate. (D. Venter)

Moffel MPV (right). Sandstone Heritage Estate. (D. Venter)

Moffel MPV (front left). Sandstone Heritage Estate. (D. Venter)

Cargo Carrier

Based on the Buffel Mk1B, the Cargo Carrier variant was produced in the early 1980s. It retained the standard one-man driver's cab, but the personnel tub was replaced with an open load bed, allowing it to carry up to 2.6t of cargo over a range of 900km (559mi). A total of 57 Cargo Carrier variants were produced.

Ambulance

The Ambulance variant was a prototype based on the Buffel Mk1B. It retained the armoured one-man driver's cab, while the passenger tub was redesigned to be enclosed. The ambulance could accommodate two medical staff, four lying patients, and one sitting patient. Access to the tub was gained through a rear door. However, the vehicle's swaying motion, inherent in the Buffel's design, made it difficult and uncomfortable to treat casualties while in transit. Additionally, the modifications added 400kg (882lbs) to the vehicle's weight, which was deemed unacceptable for the chassis. As a result, no orders were placed for this variant.

Mine Incidents and Non-Contact Accidents

The Buffel's primary role was to protect its occupants from the deadly threat of landmine blasts, which were a constant danger in the operational areas where the vehicle was deployed. Table 1 demonstrates the Buffel's success in fulfilling this critical role, showcasing its ability to safeguard soldiers and minimise casualties in mine-related incidents and non-contact accidents.

Table 1: Certified Buffel mine incidents

Mine type	Incidents	Killed	Injured	Personnel
Single mines (6kg [13lbs] TNT)	206	9	326	-
Double mines (12kg [26lbs] TNT)	34	10	111	-
Triple mines (18kg [39lbs] TNT)	6	2	16	-
Total number	246	19	453	2,706
Total percentage		0.007%	5.97%	

Brigadier General (retd) Tony Savides puts the Buffel into perspective:

At the time Buffel was acquired, it was pretty much in line with (then) existing MPV technology and design, i.e. a mine-and ballistic-protected body upon a B-vehicle chassis. A V-shape and height above the blast were key elements of the technology at the time. The monocoque MPVs such as Casspir, Mamba and others came later. The only other section-carrying MPV in SADF series use at that stage was the Hippo; while there were also a number of Bosvark MPVs in service (the latter not exactly meeting the then criteria for MPVs).

The initial role for which MPVs (and thus Buffel) was intended was the protection of an infantry section (or equivalent) on roads in areas where vehicle (or tank) mines and ambushes were a threat. All-wheel or off-road drive was a secondary requirement for (a) poor to bad roads and (b) emergency travel off-road – such as in counter-ambush drills and follow-up. Buffel was thus "mine and ambush-protected" and not intended as anything more than a patrol vehicle. The rationale behind the "on roads" use was that, with the exception of minefields and random "nuisance mines", mines were pre-eminently planted on roads used by military personnel and civilians.

However, Buffel's capabilities were such that it was soon being employed in an "aggressive APC role" over and above the more-passive "mine defence role"; and the MPV was used extensively in several cross-border operations in concert with Ratels and later Casspirs. This will, hopefully, one day be the subject of a study and/or a book on the role of the MPVs in the Border War.

The requirement for a more capable MPV was identified almost as Buffel was coming into service and I personally wrote the staff requirement for the "Mine-protected Combat Vehicle" (MPCV) – in essence, a replacement for Buffel in certain roles and to provide a better combat capability. This requirement was binned when Casspir was acquired, and it re-surfaced later as part of other projects; but to date, this requirement has not been satisfied (if it still exists at all). Buffel was retained due to its proven effectiveness.

The acquisition of the Mamba 4x2 and later the conversion of Mamba into a 4x4 using Unimog/Buffel components was a direct result of different APC types being required for internal security operations.

That Buffel may have been used outside its intended role is accepted; but this should have been mitigated by proper training, effective command and control and effective discipline. In many, if not most, photographs of Buffels deployed and moving on roads; there are personnel standing in the back – some even standing on the seats.

The Buffel having a high centre had a dubious reputation for falling over. There were 59 such incidents which resulted in 72 deaths. Some of the possible causes:

- High centre of gravity
- Body roll at speed, especially on overtaking or when taking evasive action
- Instability caused by personnel in the rear standing instead of being seated
- Instability increased if standing persons moved around
- Speed (higher than safe for the conditions and/or in contravention of SOPs and other orders)
- Reckless driving (too-sharp turns at speed, unnecessary swerving, excessive braking, etc.)
- Showing off by drivers
- Inexperienced drivers and/or commanders
- Inclement weather
- Off-road tyres that grip in a sideways skid on hard roads (rather than slide over the surface)
- Mechanical failures (e.g. one recorded incidents of a wheel coming off on the move)
- Poor maintenance
- Under-inflated tyres
- Slippery road surfaces (wet or dusty)
- Different tyre types on a vehicle

- Poor discipline
- Poor command and control
- Heavy items not secured in the hull and which became projectiles on rollover. (Obviously, in certain states or readiness some items had to be free to use)
- It is accepted that contact or follow-up drills may have required speeding-up, swerving and personnel leaving their seats to carry out certain actions. Roll-overs may well have occurred during such actions

Operational History

During the South African Border War, the Buffel served as a dedicated transport vehicle for infantry, as well as a platform for logistics and COIN operations. Deployed as part of combat groups, the Buffel transported infantry sections to designated points, from which they would dismount and conduct foot patrols lasting between three and seven days. After this, they would either be picked up or resupplied for an additional seven days.

A typical fighting group consisted of between four to six Buffels, transporting a full platoon. One or two of these vehicles served as supply and logistics vehicles, carrying sufficient food, water, and ammunition for seven days, allowing for a range of 600–800km (373–497mi). In cases of extended patrols, replenishment was conducted every six days to ensure the group's operational endurance.

Buffel. (HR Heitman)

A soldier's story with the Buffel – 31/201BN – OPS PROTEA – "LANDMINE(S)"
17 August 1981

We were travelling between someplace and somewhere (memory a bit sketchy!) in convoy, trying to get to one of our key destinations. The convoy was stretched for kilometres, snaking through the hot bush and sand of Southern Angola.

At some point, a substantial gap opened up within the convoy, and I was radioed to wait for the stragglers. My Buffel, call sign 33A, named *"Brits-Tax Racing"* by my young, new, enthusiastic driver (from somewhere near Pietermaritzburg, KwaZulu-Natal), peeled off and took some shelter under a large Mopani tree, together with Buffel 33B, waiting for the convoy members behind us to catch up. The gap must have been around a kilometre long. We waited until the rest caught up and then proceeded to follow in the substantial track left by the convoy in front of us. We travelled approximately two to three kilometres when, all of a sudden, all hell seemed to break loose.

I remember standing behind the driver's cab, trying to direct him, when one almighty "bang" blew the 16-ton Buffel into the air and onto its left side, the back wheel landing in the hole left by the cheese mine that blew the left front wheel and tyre right off the vehicle. Dust, sand, fumes, and confusion reigned for a few seconds, after which we all de-bussed and did a *rondom verdediging* (all-round defence).

I was dazed and slightly confused from the blast, with my knuckles sandblasted by the sand coming through the gap between the cab and the '*bak*' (passenger tub). My eyes were bloodshot from the dust, and my hearing was totally screwed. To add insult to injury, I managed to smack my left shoulder into the roll bar in the middle of the vehicle! Must have been some serious acrobatic move! At a much later stage, this shoulder also needed corrective surgery, as the tendons had calcified and hardened from the impact with the roll bar, and had to be cut, shortened, and reattached.

Clearly, at some stage within the gap in the convoy, SWAPO decided to plant this mine, and we managed to detonate it. Little did we know that this would not be the last mine detonated for the day!

With one mortally wounded Buffel, my section waited for one of the supply Kwevoels to pick us up and take us further on our journey. On the back of the transporter, lying on top of the unit's kit, rats (rations), etc., we baked in the sun, and with my hearing totally shot, I was yelling and shouting at everyone to much of their amusement.

We caught up with the rest of the convoy shortly later, at which time Lt. Swazi Naudé promptly detonated a mine with another Buffel. He then proceeded to climb into a second Buffel, travelled a few metres, and promptly detonated yet another mine! Not even two or three minutes later, Kmdt. Frans Botes then summarily detonated a fourth mine, at which point all decided to "relax" and assess the situation. It was later found that we had driven into a minefield left behind by SWAPO.

The Sappers, bless their nerves of steel, proceeded to lift around sixty mines, as well as a few anti-personnel mines.

From this episode, the unit acquired a section of Swazi's rim and made the *"Crackerjack Trophy."* This trophy can still be seen at the McGregor Museum in Kimberley.

We plotted on and eventually reached Ongiva, at which time I was told to get ready to be casevaced. Clearly, my inability

to hear caused some concern, and I think that between the three of us we were using up all the sterile water and eye drops trying to wash the dust out of our eyes.

I was bundled into a DC-3 Dakota leaving for Ondangwa and then caught a *Flossie* (C-130 Hercules) all the way to Waterkloof Air Force Base, Pretoria. With my full bush kit (rifle, webbing, ammo, kit, etc.) and dirty as all hell from weeks in the bush, I arrived at 1 Military Hospital. The surgeon examined me and promptly said that there was nothing they could do right then (I think it was a Friday morning) and that I should report back on the Monday.

There I stood dirty, smelly, all my kit and thought, "what now?"

Then I remembered that an old school friend of mine, Karen Jacobs, was in residence at RAU (Rand Afrikaans University), so I promptly hitchhiked to Johannesburg and walked into her residence, waiting in the foyer for her appearance (remember, this was long before cell phones!). I must have been a sight for sore eyes, as everyone stared at me and gave me a wide berth (must have been my deodorant?). About an hour later, she arrived, and we went to a nearby shop to get some slip-ons, a pair of jeans, and a T-shirt. After a good long hot shower at a friend's place, dressed in my new clobber, we took on the weekend!

Monday, back at the hospital, I was once again informed that there was nothing they could do immediately, and that we should see if the eardrums would not grow closed by themselves. So, back I went to the air base and flew back to Omega on the next available plane.

As it turned out, my right eardrum did close up by itself, but the left had to be replaced with an artificial "plastic" eardrum. Both operations took place after I *klaared* out (completed service), at the new 1 Military Hospital in Pretoria.

2nd Lt D. Van Den Berg

Conclusion

The Buffel is the world's first mass-produced, V-shaped hull, mine-protected vehicle, designed to safeguard personnel during the height of the South African Border War. While its open-topped configuration and limited comfort often drew criticism from those who used it, the Buffel's primary mission was protection and in that, it excelled. Its ability to withstand landmine blasts saved the lives of countless SADF soldiers operating in mine-riddled terrain, making it the backbone of SADF border patrols and COIN operations.

Throughout its 17 years of service, the Buffel demonstrated unmatched reliability in various roles, including transport, logistics, and direct engagement support. As military technology advanced, the Buffel's limitations in terms of protection from modern weapons and its lack of comfort became more pronounced. This led to its gradual replacement by the more advanced Mamba MPV in 1995. However, the legacy of the Buffel endures. Its design principles influenced future generations of mine-protected vehicles, and more than 582 Buffels were repurposed and rebuilt using its driveline to form the foundation of the Mamba fleet.

The Buffel's role in the evolution of military vehicle design cannot be understated. Its innovative design set the standard for mine protection when such technology was in its infancy. Although retired, its contributions continue to be acknowledged in military circles worldwide, particularly in conflict regions that have adopted similar mine-resistant designs.

Buffel 33A post mine detonation. (D. Van Den Berg)

3

Ratel Infantry Combat Vehicle

The Ratel ICV was a groundbreaking design created to provide rapid mobility and heavy firepower to the mechanised infantry units of the SADF. Introduced during a time when the SADF required vehicles capable of performing efficiently in the vast and varied terrain of Southern Africa, the Ratel quickly became an indispensable asset in military operations, particularly during the South African Border War. Its unique combination of firepower, versatility, and endurance on the battlefield allowed it to serve as a key component of the SADF's combat forces for over three decades.

The Ratel's design reflected the specific challenges of bush warfare in Southern Africa, emphasising mobility, durability, and the ability to carry and support infantry in fast-moving, dynamic combat situations. Whether navigating rugged terrain or engaging in long-range operations, the Ratel was essential to the SADF's mechanised units, providing protection and firepower in a variety of combat scenarios.

Development

In the mid-1960s, the SADF realised that foreign-imported armoured troop carriers, such as the Saracen, were not up to the task against modern threats and did not meet the specific requirements of the southern African battlespace. What was needed was a highly manoeuvrable, ultra-reliable, and easy-to-maintain ICV that could provide substantial firepower while meeting the growing demands of mobile warfare. This vision led to the inception of *Project Pampoen* (Pumpkin), which would eventually result in the development of the Ratel ICV. The formal user requirement for the vehicle was finalised in 1970.

In 1972, Springfield Büssing, a South African company, presented a 6x6 APC built by MAN for evaluation. This vehicle would later be named the Buffel (not to be confused with the Buffel MPV from Chapter 2). After a series of trials, the Springfield Büssing Buffel was found to be the most suitable design and, following another year of evaluation and trials, was selected as the developmental platform for the Ratel.

The first prototype, the Ratel SS, was made from mild steel, which allowed for easier modifications during testing. While the Ratel SS shared some external resemblance with the Buffel, it was a completely different design in terms of functionality and capability. Testing of the Ratel SS took place over a five-month period in 1974, after which the first four production Ratel's underwent rigorous field trials at Elandsfontein vehicle testing grounds near Pretoria in 1975.

In 1975, the first batch of 13 Ratel Mk1 vehicles was delivered from the production line at Sandock-Austral in Boksburg, followed by mass production. Based on operational feedback, several modifications were made to improve the Ratel's performance in the bush. These included adding large covers to protect external headlights (which were originally covered by mesh wire) and installing a screen cover to prevent leaves from entering the engine. These changes, which enhanced the Ratel's bush-breaking capability, were later designated as the Mk3 standard.

The Ratel 20, the base model of the Ratel family, formed the foundation for the subsequent variants. In 1979/1980, after successful evaluation and testing, production began for the Ratel 12.7 Command variant. In 1974, the need for an anti-tank vehicle was identified, and by early 1979, an Eland 90 turret was mounted on a strengthened Ratel 20 hull, creating the Ratel 90. After successful live-fire tests, the Ratel 90 was ordered for production and saw its first combat during Operation Sceptic as part of Battle Group 61.

In 1980/1981, the Ratel 60 was conceived as a temporary solution due to a shortage of Ratel 20s, which was caused by a lack of available 20mm F2 GIAT guns. The Ratel 60 was quickly produced by fitting an Eland 60 turret on a Ratel 20 hull, a process that only took about an hour.

Ratel variants (left to right) Ratel 90, Ratel 12.7, Ratel 81, Ratel 60, Ratel ZT3A1 and Ratel 20. (Reumech OMC)

Springfield Büssing. 1 SAI Battalion. (D. Venter)

Ratel SS. 1 SAI Battalion. (D. Venter)

Ratel 0003 (left) and 0002 (right) immediately prior to leaving Sandock-Austral for the evaluation in May 1975. (T. Savides)

Work on the Ratel 81 began in 1983 after the cancellation of a similar project with similar capabilities. The Ratel 81 was delivered in mid-1985, with its first operational deployment during Operation Benzine. In the early 1960s, the need for a mobile anti-tank missile capability was recognised, which led to the acquisition of Milan AT missiles in the mid-1970s. However, these wire-guided missiles proved impractical in the African bush, where the guiding wire would frequently become tangled in foliage, and targets could easily move out of sight before the missile hit. This prompted the development of a domestic, laser-guided missile system, which was completed by Kentron in 1986. The newly developed ZT3 missile system was mounted on a Ratel 20 hull with a specially designed turret.

The Ratel Mk3 standard, introduced in 1985, included over 135 modifications, such as an improved cooling system, additional fuel filters, a digital acceleration meter, and more robust protection against the bush, including relocating the exterior lights lower on the vehicle and reinforcing the entry steps.

As the South African Border War escalated, the Ratel family was pivotal in providing the SADF with the necessary mobility and firepower. From 1976 onward, as cross-border operations became more frequent, Ratel formations were often used in battalion-sized columns, supported by other South African military vehicles such as the Buffel, Eland, and SAMIL vehicles. The Ratel was employed to intercept SWAPO raiders crossing the border into South West Africa and was frequently used in long-range incursions into Angola.

As the conflict escalated, Cuban troops and Soviet advisors intervened in support of the MPLA and FAPLA, but the SADF's doctrine of mobile warfare coupled with the Ratel's high mobility and firepower allowed them to outmanoeuvre numerically superior opponents. The Ratel family of vehicles proved essential in achieving tactical superiority during these operations.

Since its introduction in 1974, the Ratel family formed the backbone of SADF's mechanised operations throughout the South African Border War. It was deployed by several units, including 61 Mech, 32 Bn, 4 and 8 SAI Battalions, and even Citizen Force Mechanised Infantry units. It also served other branches of the SADF, such as artillery, engineers, and signals. The Ratel continued to be in service after the SADF transitioned into the SANDF and was used in the 1998 Southern African Development Community (SADC) intervention in Lesotho, led by the SANDF. Additionally, UN peacekeeping forces have employed the Ratel in various conflict zones.

In total, 1,381 Ratels were built, and since 1994, Ratels have been exported to several countries, including Cameroon, Djibouti, Ghana, Jordan, Libya, Morocco, Rwanda, Sahrawi Arab Democratic Republic, Senegal, Yemen, and Zambia. Exported Ratels have seen action during the Libyan Civil War, the Yemeni Revolution, and Yemeni Civil War.

Design Features

The Ratel was the best vehicle ever made for the ultra-mobile African bush warfare. The terrain it operated in is some of the most hostile in the world, which alone inflicts harsh punishment. Characterised by its massive wheels, swiftness, bush breaking ability and versatility as a weapons platform, it was a fearsome adversary in skilled hands during the South African Border War.

Major General (retd) Roland de Vries

Mobility

The Ratel is a 6x6 wheeled vehicle, designed for exceptional versatility and cross-country capability, specifically optimised for the harsh and varied terrain of the African battlespace. It is equipped with 14:00x20 run-flat tyres, designed to resist the effects of deflation in the event of a puncture, allowing the vehicle to maintain mobility in hostile environments.

The Ratel is powered by the Büssing D 3256 BTXF six-cylinder direct-injection turbocharged diesel engine, which delivers 282hp (210kW) at 2,400rpm, providing a 14.9hp/t power-to-weight ratio for the Ratel 20. This engine, located at the rear left of the vehicle, proved more than sufficient to navigate off-road terrain, pushing through dense bush and small trees with ease. The power pack is designed for rapid field maintenance, and the engine can be field stripped and replaced in approximately 30 minutes by two men using a crane.

The engine is coupled to an automatic powershift gearbox, which includes a hydrodynamic torque converter, making driving smoother and more efficient. While the gearbox operates automatically, it also has the option for manual operation and a mechanical emergency gearshift. Gear selection includes five forward gears, a neutral position, and two reverse gears. Power is transmitted to the three axles in two stages, with a final reduction achieved using planetary gearing located in the wheel hubs. Each of the three axles is equipped with its own lockable differential, and there are longitudinal differential locks for added traction on difficult terrain.

The suspension system utilises progressive coil springs and large hydraulic shock absorbers, which provide the Ratel with stability and comfort when traversing rugged landscapes. The vehicle has a 350mm (13.8in) ground clearance and can ford 1.2m (3.9ft) of water unprepared. However, early trials humorously revealed that the Ratel, though not amphibious, kept the engine running underwater until it was rescued, an impressive testament to its durability.

While the Ratel is not built for amphibious operations, it can perform well in diverse environments, sometimes even becoming semi-airborne though this will be detailed in another publication. The maximum recommended safe road speed is 80km/h (50mph), though it can reach speeds of 120km/h (75mph) unofficially. Depending on terrain, the Ratel can achieve 40km/h (25mph) cross-country. It is also capable of crossing a 1.15m (3.8ft) ditch at a crawl and can climb a 60% gradient, showcasing its impressive mobility in even the most challenging conditions.

The Ratel is equipped with three beam axles, coil springs, and shock absorbers, all contributing to its ability to operate effectively in the toughest environments.

Endurance and logistics

The Ratel is equipped with a 480ℓ (37.5gal) fuel tank, providing it with an impressive range of 1,000km (621mi) on-road and 600km (372mi) off-road. This fuel capacity allows for flexible movement, enabling the Ratel to operate independently and achieve the element of surprise during operations.

Some Ratel variants were equipped with three 7.62mm BMG, one mounted co-axially to the left of the primary weapon, another positioned on the turret structure above the commander's station for close protection against ground threats, and a third mounted on the right rear of the hull for close-in anti-air support. However, most Ratels were fitted with just the coaxial and commander's station BMG. The AA mount, initially intended for anti-air defence, was found to be ineffective in that role and was later repurposed for close-in ground defence. On average, a Ratel carried at least 6,000 rounds of 7.62mm BMG ammunition for its various armaments.

For tactical communication, the Ratel is equipped with both B-56 long-range and B-26 short-range radios, located at the rear of the turret. These communication systems enabled reliable command and control, enhancing the Ratel's effectiveness as a force multiplier on the battlefield. During the South African Border War, effective communication between Ratel 90s allowed SADF crews to successfully engage and destroy T-54/55 MBTs across multiple operations.

The Ratel is also equipped with two built-in drinking water tanks, holding a total of 100ℓ (26gal) of water. Additional jerry cans for extra water were carried based on operational requirements and stored wherever space permitted.

Designed to operate over rugged and unpredictable terrain with minimal logistical support, the Ratel is self-sustaining, carrying its own supplies, some spare parts, and a section of infantry. Spare wheels were often lashed to the roof of the hull, while food supplies were stored in every available compartment, often including a few cases of beer. To ensure continuous operation, spare whip aerials for the radios were also carried, as they had a tendency to break when driving through dense brush. The overall emphasis was on self-sufficiency the Ratel could provide its own fire support, perform first aid, and continue operations independently for up to three days without external supply.

Vehicle layout

The Ratel holds the distinction of being the first wheeled ICV to ever be mass-produced and actively serve in combat. It is equipped with a proper commander's cupola, offering a full 360-degree field of vision for the vehicle commander. The commander is seated on the left side of the turret, while the gunner occupies the right side. The commander and gunner enter and exit the vehicle through their respective hatches. In case of an emergency, both can escape through the rear of the vehicle, ensuring a quick and safe exit.

The driver's compartment is located at the front and centre of the vehicle, offering the driver an excellent 270-degree view through three large bulletproof windows. For additional protection during battle, the driver can activate three armoured shields, which deploy to cover the windows. When these shields are in place, the driver uses three day-periscopes for vision to the front, left, and right. The driver has two options for entry and exit: through a roof hatch above his seat or from within the vehicle itself.

The driver's controls include a hydraulically-supported steering wheel, which controls the front two wheels, and foot pedals for acceleration and braking. Additionally, all Ratels are equipped with a small crane jib or tow bar at the rear for towing damaged vehicles.

The hull of the Ratel has entry doors on the left and right sides, which are operated by a hydraulic system, ensuring that the doors close securely at any angle. The rear door is manumatic, allowing for easy operation by the crew. Roof hatches are present (number depending on the specific variant), which can be used for weapon deployment, such as the firing of personal weapons and grenades, as well as for loading and emergency exit if needed.

A Ratel 20 carries a standard crew of three members: the vehicle commander, gunner, and driver. It can also carry up to eight soldiers. Although the interior is relatively crowded, additional space is available for up to three more passengers when necessary, although this is not standard practise. The mounted soldiers are seated back-to-back, allowing them to fire through several firing ports located on either side of the vehicle. To ensure safety, all seats are equipped with safety belts, preventing passengers from being thrown about during rough terrain operations.

In the Ratel 20, the section leader also serves as the vehicle commander. The vehicle is equipped with four 81mm smoke grenade launchers two on either side of the turret providing additional defensive capabilities.

Main armament

The Ratel 12.7 Command is equipped with a turret housing a 12.7mm BMG, a standard coaxial 7.62mm BMG, and an additional 7.62mm BMG mounted on top of the turret for close protection against ground threats. The vehicle typically carries 300 rounds of 12.7mm BMG ammunition.

The Ratel 20 is fitted with a dual-feed GI-2 20mm QF gun, a licenced copy of the French GIAT F2 gun, produced by Lyttelton Engineering Works (LEW, later known as Denel Land Systems) in South Africa. The primary roles of this gun are to provide sustained suppressive fire, engage enemy troops, and destroy soft-skinned and lightly armoured vehicles. The gun can elevate between -8 degrees and +38 degrees and fires at a rate of 750 rounds per minute. The auto-feed mechanism allows for easy switching between two ammunition belts, each containing 150 rounds. The primary rounds used are 20x139mm HE-I and APCT. The HE-I rounds, travelling at 1050m/s (3448ft/s), are effective up to 2km (1.2mi). The APCT rounds, with a velocity of 1,300m/s (4,265ft/s), are effective up to 1km (0.6mi) and can penetrate 15mm (0.6in) of RHA at zero degrees. The Ratel 20 carries a total of 1,200 rounds of 20mm ammunition.

The Ratel 60 is equipped with the Eland 60 turret, which retains the 60mm M2 breech-loading gun-mortar and the standard coaxial 7.62mm BMG. The 60mm mortar can fire a 1.72kg (3.8lbs) bomb at 200m/s (656ft/s), effective up to 300m (328yd) in the direct role and 2km (1.2mi) in the indirect role. The 60mm mortar is capable of firing HE, canister, smoke, and illumination rounds, with a total of 45 mortar bombs carried on board. The gun's elevation range is from -11 to +75 degrees.

The Ratel 81 is equipped with an 81mm mortar, which fires through a roof hatch located in the centre of the vehicle. The 81mm mortar is mounted on a turntable, allowing it to traverse a full 360 degrees. If needed, the mortar can be removed and used outside the vehicle. The Ratel 81 carries 148 mortar bombs, with the capacity to carry additional ammunition in external containers.

The Ratel 90 uses the same turret and 90mm GT-2 gun as the Eland 90. The 90mm gun can fire HEAT-T, HE, and canister rounds. The HEAT-T round travels at 760 m/s (2,493ft/s), with an effective range of 1.2km (0.8mi) and can penetrate up to 320mm (12.6in) of RHA at zero degrees and 150mm (5.9in) at a 60-degree angle. The HE round, weighing 5.27kg (11.6lbs), travels at 650m/s (2,133ft/s) and is accurate up to 2.2km (1.36mi). The 90mm gun can elevate between -8 degrees and +15 degrees and can rotate a full 360 degrees in 25 seconds. It carries 72 rounds of 90mm ammunition, a significant improvement over the Eland 90.

The Ratel ZT3-A1 is equipped with the ZT3A1 Swift missile, which was marketed internationally as the ZT3. The Swift missile (also known as the Mongol during development) has a minimum range of 250m (273yd) and a maximum standoff range of 4km (2.5mi). It travels at a maximum speed of 240m/s (787ft/s) and features a shaped charge capable of penetrating 600mm (23.62in) of RHA at zero degrees. The Ratel ZT3-A2 can also fire the newer ZT3A2 Ingwe (Leopard) missile, marketed as the ZT35 internationally. The Ingwe missile has the same minimum range but a standoff range of over 5km (3.1mi). It travels at 342m/s (1,122ft/s) and features a tandem warhead designed to defeat explosive reactive armour. The Ingwe can penetrate up to 1,000mm (39.37in) of RHA at zero degrees and uses laser beam riding to reach its target, making it highly resistant to jamming. The Ratel ZT3 missile system is mounted on a modified Ratel 60 turret and carries three ready-to-use missiles in the vehicle, with a total of 12 missiles carried inside the hull. These missiles are manually loaded into the tubes through the Ratel's roof hatch.

Fire control system

The Ratel 12.7, Ratel 20, Ratel 60, and Ratel 90 all use the Eloptro x5.9 magnification gunner's day sight for aiming and targeting their main armament. The main armament is aimed and laid using a hand-crank system, with sighting provided by a telescopic sight linked directly to the main gun. Due to the absence of a turret drive system, the main armament is not stabilised, requiring the gunners to manually adjust aim during movement. In the context of combat, especially during the South African Border War, this placed a high demand on the gunners' skills, as they had to work in concert to engage enemy targets quickly while minimising their exposure and withdrawing swiftly before becoming vulnerable to counterattack.

The ZT3-A1 and ZT3-A2 variants are the only Ratel models equipped with an electric turret drive, which enables automatic rotation and elevation adjustments. While specific details on the rotation speed and elevation arcs are not available, the turret drive significantly enhances targeting capabilities compared to the manually operated systems of other Ratel variants. The gunner in these variants uses a dual control stick target tracking system to guide the ZT3 missile to its target. For optical and digital magnification, it is reasonable to assume that the ZT3-A1 uses at least an Eloptro x6 sight.

In the ZT3-A1, targeting is conducted through the traditional gunner's sight, while in the ZT3-A2, the gunner operates a digital monitor for more precise targeting. Additionally, the ZT3-A1 is equipped with night vision sights, enhancing its capabilities in low-light conditions, while the ZT3-A2 features second-generation thermal sights, providing superior target acquisition capabilities in all weather and lighting conditions.

Protection

The Ratel was designed with speed and mobility as its primary focus, prioritising these characteristics over heavy armour. This made the vehicle highly effective in rapid manoeuvres but also left it vulnerable to certain threats.

The Ratel's armour consists of several layers with varying thickness across different parts of the vehicle. The lower nose plate is 20mm (0.79in) thick and is angled at 30 degrees, while the upper nose is 10mm (0.39in) thick and angled at 75 degrees. The upper hull sides are 8mm (0.31in) thick at a 25-degree angle, and the lower hull is 10mm (0.39in). The rear hull is also 10mm (0.39in) thick, with the top hull measuring 6mm (0.24in) and the hull floor at 8mm (0.31in).

The frontal arc protects against 12.7mm AP rounds, although the upper hull cheeks remain vulnerable to penetration. The rest of the hull offers sufficient protection against shrapnel and 7.62mm AP rounds. However, the Ratel was particularly susceptible to fire from Russian-supplied 23mm anti-aircraft weapons, which were often used in a ground defence role by MPLA and Cuban forces during the South African Border War.

Contrary to popular belief, the Ratel was not equipped with a V-shaped underbelly, which is commonly associated with mine-resistant vehicles. Instead, its mine resistance was primarily derived from the height of the hull above the ground, which was made possible by its large oversized wheels. These wheels were designed to blow off upon detonation, dispersing some of the explosive energy. Additionally, the wheel arches were shaped in a V-pattern, which helped deflect mine blasts and mitigate the damage to the vehicle.

During the South African Border War, only one Ratel mine fatality was recorded. This occurred when a Ratel drove over a double anti-tank mine during Operation Meebos, which detonated beneath the vehicle, resulting in a tragic loss.

The Ratel Family

The Ratel vehicle platform served as the foundation for an entire family of ICVs that have formed the backbone of the South African mechanised armed forces. This versatile platform led to the development of multiple variants, including the Ratel 12.7, Ratel 20, Ratel 60, Ratel 90, Ratel 81, Ratel 120 (prototype), Ratel ZT-3, Ratel Ambulance (field modification), Ratel Log (prototype), Ratel EAOS, Ratel EW (field modification), and the Ratel Recovery (field modification). These vehicles played a critical role in a variety of combat, logistical, and support missions throughout the South African Border War and beyond.

Ratel 12.7 Command

The Ratel 12.7 is equipped with a 12.7mm main weapon, allowing for a more spacious turret interior compared to the Ratel 20. The vehicle typically carries a three-man crew the vehicle commander, driver, and main gunner with space to accommodate six command post personnel. The troop compartment is outfitted with map tables and communication equipment, fulfilling its intended role for command and control. To ensure reliable operation, particularly for the additional communications equipment, the Ratel 12.7 is fitted with an air-conditioning system to prevent overheating. Other variants of this model include the Ratel 20 Command and the Ratel 60 Command.

Ratel 12.7 at General De Wet shooting range. (J. Van Zyl)

Ratel 20

The Ratel 20 also carries a three-man crew, with space for anywhere from eight to 11 mounted infantry, depending on mission requirements. Designed with a focus on rapid offensive operations, it plays a critical role in closing with and destroying the enemy through mobility and firepower. As part of its strategic utility, the Ratel 20 was later adapted to Irish Army service, where Reumech supplied Ratel 20 turrets to be mounted on their AML vehicles.

Ratel 60

The Ratel 60 is typically assigned to an AC troop for fire support and anti-ambush duties. Unlike the more direct-fire focused variants, the Ratel 60 most often operates from the rear, providing indirect fire support to advancing forces. Its 60mm mortar makes it a valuable asset for long-range suppression and area denial.

Ratel 20 at AAD 2024. (D. Venter)

Ratel 60 at AAD 2024. (D. Venter)

Ratel 81

The first four prototypes of the Ratel 81 were delivered to 1 SAI on 12 November 1985. Unlike other Ratel variants, the Ratel 81 does not feature a turret. Instead, it is equipped with a commander's cupola where the turret would typically be located. This version has two firing ports on either side of the vehicle, designed for personal weapons and self-defence.

The Ratel 81 carries a standard three-man crew the vehicle commander, driver, and gunner and includes a three-man mortar team. It operates primarily within a combat group to provide indirect fire support using shoot and scoot tactics, which involve quick firing followed by immediate relocation to avoid counterfire. The Ratel 81 is particularly effective in mobile warfare where flexibility and rapid repositioning are crucial.

Ratel 90

The Ratel 90 is based on the Ratel 20 platform but is equipped with a 90mm low-velocity GT-2 gun, similar to the Eland 90 it replaced. This vehicle is primarily used for anti-tank and fire support roles. The Ratel 90 provides enhanced firepower over the Ratel 20, making it a versatile weapon in engaging both lightly armoured vehicles and infantry while supporting infantry operations with its heavy firepower.

Further modifications to the Ratel 90 involved a reworking of the roof lining and a reduction in the number of troop compartment roof hatches from four to two. This change was made to accommodate the turret overhang, optimising space and improving the vehicle's operational efficiency. The Ratel 90 also carries only one additional crew member in mechanised infantry units, while there are no extra

Ratel 81 at SA Armour Museum Open Day 2024. (D. Venter)

Ratel 90 at SA Armour Musuem Open Day 2024. (D. Venter)

crew members in AC units. This reconfiguration creates additional space for ammunition racks, allowing for the storage of more rounds for the 90mm main gun.

During the South African Border War, it proved to be a formidable match for the T-34/85 tanks encountered in the early stages of the conflict. As the war progressed, FAPLA began receiving more advanced Soviet-made tanks, including the T-54/55 and T-62. By 1981, these new threats required the Ratel 90 crews to adapt their tactics.

Mechanised infantry groups equipped with the Ratel 90 demonstrated exceptional skill in outmanoeuvring the newer Soviet tanks, often engaging them from advantageous positions. To successfully disable the T-54/55 and T-62 tanks, the Ratel 90 crews would frequently need to achieve multiple hits with 90mm HEAT rounds, targeting vulnerable points such as engine vents and turret rings. These tactics allowed the Ratel 90 to neutralise otherwise superior tank threats, proving its worth in the evolving conflict.

Ratel 120. (Stefan Nell)

Ratel 120

The Ratel 120 is a modified version of the Ratel 81, fitted with a 120mm mortar. The modifications required for this version were minimal. Successful tests conducted in 1993 at Alkantpan confirmed that the 120mm mortar, even when firing at maximum charge, did not adversely affect the Ratel's suspension system. Despite its success in tests, no Ratel 120 vehicles were produced beyond the prototype stage, and it remains a unique, experimental version of the Ratel family.

Ratel ZT3

The Ratel ZT3 is a dedicated anti-armour, support, and reconnaissance vehicle, equipped with the Ingwe missile system developed under Project Raleigh. In the face of international sanctions, the SADF lacked a missile system capable of effectively engaging modern MBTs. The Ingwe missile system was developed to fill this gap, and the Ratel ZT3 became the platform for South Africa's first truly modern anti-tank missile system.

The Ratel ZT3 made its combat debut in September 1987 during Operation Moduler, even before it was fully in production. Four pre-production Ratel ZT3 vehicles were assigned to 32 Bn. In a notable engagement, one of these vehicles successfully destroyed three MBTs at a distance of 2,000m in just 10 minutes, demonstrating the effectiveness of the new missile system.

In 2005, the SANDF upgraded 13 ZT3-A1 vehicles to the ZT3-A2 standard as part of Project Adrift. The upgraded vehicles feature enhanced capabilities, including the ability to fire both the Ingwe and Swift missile, making the ZT3-A2 highly versatile. The ZT3-A1 launcher is compatible only with the Swift missile.

Ratel ZT3-A2. (C. Hugo)

The Ratel ZT3-A1 is equipped with night vision sights for the gunner, while the ZT3-A2 is equipped with thermal imaging, maximising its effectiveness during night-time operations and improving its lethality against enemy armour. As of the present day, approximately 40 ZT3 vehicles remain in service, continuing to provide the SANDF with a potent anti-tank capability.

Ratel Ambulance

The Ratel Ambulance was initially part of the official Ratel project but was ultimately developed as a field modification. The first operational deployment occurred during operations Reindeer and Sceptic. The Ratel Ambulance was based on a converted Ratel 20 hull and was equipped for medical trauma support, carrying the necessary medical equipment to treat and evacuate casualties in combat situations. While not a dedicated production variant, the Ratel Ambulance proved invaluable for casualty evacuation and support during the conflict.

Ratel Logistic

Unlike the other Ratel variants, the Ratel Log was designed as an 8x8 wheeled vehicle, enabling it to keep pace with the mechanised family of Ratel vehicles while providing logistical support. The Ratel Log was intended to carry sufficient supplies to support a Ratel platoon for up to one week during high-intensity operations, or two weeks for low-intensity operations. While around 100 Ratel Log vehicles were ordered, the project was ultimately cancelled due to budget restraints, and none were produced. Had it been produced, the Ratel Log would have been a vital component in sustaining mechanised forces during prolonged engagements.

Ratel Enhanced Observation and Surveillance

The Ratel Enhanced Observation and Surveillance (EAOS) vehicle features a distinctive design with no turret and a hydraulically operated mast. When raised, the mast reaches a height of 30m (98ft), providing a high vantage point while keeping the vehicle protected. The mast is equipped with an advanced sensor package, including a video camera system for both day and night use, a long-range zoom lens, a forward looking infrared (FLIR) viewer, a laser designator, and a laser rangefinder with an integrated video channel.

This sophisticated system allows the Ratel EAOS to perform accurate target observation at ranges of up to 20km (12.4mi) during the day, and up to 3.5km (2.2mi) at night. A vehicle-mounted computer system processes the incoming data and computes the necessary firing solutions for artillery units. The Ratel EAOS is a crucial asset for the SANDF Artillery Arm, enabling precise target identification and coordination for effective fire support.

Ratel EW

In the latter stages of the South African Border War, a significant need arose for dedicated electronic warfare (EW) capabilities to support forward operations. In response, the SADF converted several Ratel vehicles to carry EW equipment, which was crucial for disrupting enemy communications and command and control systems. The Ratel EW variant was equipped with specialised systems designed to interfere with enemy electronic systems, ensuring that the SADF maintained operational superiority in the electronic battlefield.

Ratel Recovery

The Ratel Recovery was a field modification introduced during Operation Reindeer, based on a modified Ratel 20 hull. It was fitted with a recovery frame designed to assist in the recovery of damaged vehicles from the battlefield. This modification allowed Ratel Recovery vehicles to support mechanised operations by towing or recovering disabled vehicles, ensuring that critical assets remained operational and reducing downtime for SADF units during combat.

Operational History

The Ratel ICV played an essential and transformative role in the operational history of the SADF during the South African Border War, particularly in cross-border operations between 1978 and 1989. Designed initially for conventional warfare, the Ratel's versatility

Ratel Logistic at 1 SAI. (D. Venter)

and adaptability allowed it to fulfil various roles, including infantry transport, fire support, reconnaissance, and anti-tank operations, making it the backbone of the SADF's mechanised infantry.

The Ratel formed the backbone of all significant cross-border operations undertaken by the SADF. Military historian Leopold Scholtz affirms that without the Ratel, 'no single cross-border operation of any significance' would have been possible, with the exception of the airborne assault on Cassinga. He points out that operations like Sceptic, Protea, Daisy, Moduler, Hooper, and Packer relied heavily on the Ratel's presence, and its absence would have significantly altered the course of the war. Its effectiveness in these operations highlights the vehicle's pivotal role in the SADF's mechanised warfare strategy, particularly in long-range deep-penetration raids into Angola.

In Operation Protea, the largest deployment of Ratels (over 60) was central to the operation's success. The Ratel 90 was instrumental in neutralising Angolan tanks and providing fire support for mechanised infantry The ability of the Ratel to traverse difficult terrain and engage enemy positions over extended distances allowed the SADF to maintain mobility and flexibility throughout the operation. Protea was a decisive victory for the SADF, and the use of Ratels ensured that they could sustain prolonged engagements far from their bases.

The Ratel's versatility allowed it to perform effectively in various roles beyond its original infantry transport function. In Operation Askari, the Ratel 90 was crucial in engagements with Angolan T-54/55 tanks. Although the Ratel 90 had limitations when directly engaging heavily armoured vehicles, its tactical use in conjunction with terrain advantages enabled the SADF to hold its own against numerically superior forces.

Another notable operation was Operation Moduler, where the Ratel was deployed alongside tanks in large-scale conventional warfare. This operation demonstrated the full potential of the Ratel as a combat system, with variants like the Ratel 81 mortar carrier and the pre-production Ratel ZT-3 playing critical roles for anti-tank operations later in the conflict (see soldier's story in Chapter 3). Despite facing well-equipped Angolan and Cuban forces supported by Soviet armour, the SADF's ability to rapidly manoeuvre Ratels allowed them to maintain battlefield superiority.

The Ratel's design facilitated its operation over long distances in harsh conditions, often deep within enemy territory. Its bush protection kits, developed after early operational feedback, improved its survivability in dense bush and rugged terrains typical of Angola.

These enhancements, along with continuous modifications based on field reports, kept the Ratel relevant and effective throughout the conflict

By the end of the South African Border War, the Ratel had proven itself not just as an infantry carrier but as a multifaceted combat vehicle capable of adapting to the evolving needs of the SADF. Its reliability, ease of maintenance, and operational flexibility made it indispensable in the mechanised units, particularly 61 Mech, which became synonymous with mobile warfare in Southern Africa. The Ratel's ability to operate in diverse roles infantry support, firepower delivery, and anti-tank engagements ensured that it remained a key player in every major SADF operation.

The Ratel's operational history underscores its role as the backbone of the SADF's cross-border operations. Its versatility, coupled with the development of new tactics and mechanised doctrines around its capabilities, enabled the SADF to conduct mobile, deep-penetration raids that defined the South African Border War. From Protea to Moduler, the Ratel's presence ensured that the SADF maintained battlefield superiority, making it a symbol of South Africa's mechanised warfare doctrine.

During Operation Boleas, a military invasion launched by the SADC into Lesotho, the Ratel was extensively used by the SANDF for mechanised infantry support. A number of variants of the Ratel were deployed to patrol key areas in Maseru, Lesotho, amid widespread unrest following contested elections. The Ratel's firepower and mobility made it highly effective in urban operations, helping to restore order by engaging insurgents and securing strategic positions. Its flexibility as both a troop carrier and combat vehicle proved vital during peacekeeping efforts.

The Ratel's legacy is marked by an impressive 50 years of service, a feat that few military vehicles can rival. However, as with all technology, the Ratel has now entered its final stretch of operational service. The SANDF, through Project Hoefyster, plan on replacing one mechanised battalion's worth of Ratels with the Badger family of ICVs.

Breathing New Life into A Veteran Warhorse

The South African Ratel fleet can be upgraded through the OTT Solutions Ratel SLEP (Service Life Extension Plan) developed with ADG Mobility. The aim is to revitalise South Africa's ageing Ratels, which have served as the backbone of the mechanised infantry for decades.

First shown at AAD 2022, the demonstrator later appeared during Exercise Vuk'uhlome at Lohatla. The SLEP concept was born

Ratel SLEP. (D. Venter)

out of necessity. With Denel unable to meet the requirements of Project Hoefyster and with no clear delivery timeline, the SANDF faces a genuine risk of a capability gap. OTT Solutions proposed a cost-effective way to keep mechanised forces operational within tightening defence budgets.

The upgrade does not alter the hull or internal layout. This allows operators to field upgraded and legacy Ratels side-by-side while implementation is phased in. The centrepiece of the programme is a commercial off-the-shelf 360hp (268kW) engine paired with a six-speed automatic gearbox and a single-speed transfer case, supported by a redesigned cooling system. This modern powertrain increases output by about 30%, improving mobility, easing maintenance, and ensuring access to globally available spares.

Platform improvements extend beyond the driveline. Optional enhancements include:

- Appliqué armour for improved protection
- Upgraded braking and pneumatic systems
- Crew compartment insulation against fumes, noise, and heat
- A redesigned seating system for better ergonomics and safety
- Military-grade tyres for harsh terrain and long endurance

The upgraded vehicle retains the GI-2 20mm gun, though its effectiveness is raised through better fire control. An electrically assisted gun drive allows faster and more accurate first-round engagement. This is paired with a slaved day and night sight with a laser rangefinder for the gunner. A fully stabilised independent commander's sight is available as an option, enhancing both lethality and situational awareness and enabling hunter-killer functionality. In a future platoon layout, only the platoon commander would carry this sight, directing the sections under him.

The late General Gilbert Ramano, who championed the project as chairman of OTT Solutions, described the SLEP as a cost-effective way to keep the Ratel fleet at an acceptable operational standard. The concept has drawn interest from other African operators who face shortages of legacy Büssing engines and RENK gearboxes.

The solution has recently been evaluated by the Council for Scientific and Industrial Research (CSIR), drawing on a wide cluster of South African defence companies that contributed to the demonstrator. These include Vision 24, CC2T, Etion Create, M-Tek, Reutech Comms, SMD, Mavtech, Knoor Bremse and TFD.

Strengthening the broader South African defence industry is a lifeline for the sector. Aside from employment gains, the programme gives ARMSCOR the opportunity to sell upgraded Ratels to SADC and AU partners and create valuable export potential.

In sum, the Ratel SLEP will not turn the Ratel into a Badger, but it does offer a practical and affordable path to modernisation. It reflects a realistic understanding of the country's defence environment and provides a credible way to keep a proven combat vehicle relevant, available, and mission ready.

Conclusion

The Ratel holds the distinction of being the first true wheeled ICV to enter military service, setting a new standard for mechanised warfare globally. For its time, the Ratel was regarded as one of the best ICVs in the world, blending firepower, mobility, armour protection, and flexibility. Its design was so groundbreaking that it is considered by many military analysts to be the grandfather of all subsequent ICV designs.

Serving as the backbone of the SADF's mechanised battalions, the Ratel played a pivotal role during 12 of the 23 years of the South African Border War. The vehicle's versatility and effectiveness in a variety of combat scenarios cemented its place as an invaluable asset.

Soldier's Story – Diary of the Snakes

The following recollection is from a member of 101 Battalion, 904 SDK, Casspir call sign Romeo Mike 11.

Tuesday, 8 September 1987

We encountered 32 Battalion's camouflaged Ratels for the first time, eight Ratel 90s and four missile Ratels. Commander Hartslief was present. Our morning task was to locate a missing HIS Casspir. After a long detour, we found the contact scene: 12 FAPLA soldiers dead, one wounded survivor. One enemy soldier had attempted to crawl away when a veldfire caught up with him the heat had contorted his body into a grotesque arch, a grim reminder of war's finality.

We tracked the retreat trail and recovered both the Casspir and the recovery vehicle. FAPLA hadn't pursued. We returned with them to our TB. My vehicle suffered repeated breakdowns due to airlocks. 13A towed me back, and we replaced the diesel pump in 14C.

Later, I met Tonie Venter, a fellow Infantry School and JL alumnus. He had dropped out of VK selection, joined the Parabats, and become a pathfinder. He described the recent contact where they were attacked in a TB two days before. Tonie carried wounded men to safety under fire, earning an Honoris Crux. He gave me a camo set from a fallen 32 Bn trooper. I later learned Stuart Sterzel also received an Honoris Crux in the same engagement.

That night we drove to recon positions scouted by KM and SP another overnight trip. I struggled to sleep during the day, so it was exhausting.

Wednesday, 9 September 1987

We moved to the Lomba River and began digging in. KM remained with a Ratel company from 61 Mech, while RM11 and RM13 formed the mobile force. We patrolled west, receiving intel from UNITA about FAPLA's 21st Brigade nearby. We had a false air raid alarm we lay low under trees as MiGs passed. Once clear, we moved again and found UNITA troops who spotted two BTRs near the river, working on a mobile bridge. We advanced stealthily, halting about 300m from the BTRs. 32 Bn's Ratels struck one BTR was destroyed, the other took heavy fire. FAPLA troops scattered.

As aircraft returned, we pulled back 2km. We returned with 2Lt Pierre Liebenberg to plan a G5/MLRS strike. While observing, FAPLA and UNITA engaged nearby wild gunfire, bullets zipped overhead. We took cover. FAPLA's 21st Brigade then unleashed D-30 artillery on us, shells rained down as we retreated rapidly along the river, pursued by accurate fire for over 7km. Explosions tore up the landscape. My 14A broke a leaf spring; RM13's 20mm accidentally fired and injured several troops, though none seriously.

We regrouped and worked through the night to fix 11A's suspension. KM returned around midnight and ordered us west along the Lomba again to push the 21st Brigade, which had crossed south, back north of the river.

Thursday, 10 September 1987

We advanced in a single file through the night, later spreading into combat formation in total darkness. Casspir`s bumped into each other due to limited visibility. 904SDK led the fighting force with RM13, RM16, RM11, and SP; KM and 32 Bn followed. Around 03:00 we neared the previous day's contact area. We stopped to listen. Cpl Beyete found signs FAPLA had been there 2–3 hours earlier. We heard retreating vehicles, probably BTRs. We were ordered to dig in. A UNITA major suggested a better TB 200m ahead. RM11 and SP moved forward; RM13 and RM16 were delayed in dense bush.

Lt. Das radioed spotting two men and checked with the UNITA major, who confirmed they were friendly. Moments later, AKs opened up. They were FAPLA. Das yelled "CONTACT!" and the firefight erupted. The two imposters became the first FAPLA KIAs by 101 Bn in Operation Modular. Das re-engaged, Paulus's AA fire was deafening, and Manie's team dropped three more. Medic Blikkies grabbed an RPG tube. My driver ran over four FAPLA soldiers in the chaos.

We broke through dense bush at speed, emerging into open terrain. SP captured two; we killed another. RM13 encountered ~30 FAPLA and was hit by multiple HEAT rounds but remained operational. RM3 was immobilised. Ben from 16A collected a bayonet after shooting two enemies in quick succession. FAPLA began fleeing north across the Lomba River floodplain, totally exposed. We chased them with small arms, Brownings, and even a Patmor 60mm mortar. KM and 901 joined the barrage. The enemy was routed and psychologically broken. KM gave instructions over the radio on how to sight targets using trees across the river. Our fire was surgical. I expended 500+ rounds from both .50 and .30 cals. Snyder fired RPG-75s until the barrel glowed. RM14 got stuck at the river; 14A broke its props. One of my troops, Absalom, was hit in the thigh likely friendly fire, our only serious casualty. The contact lasted from just before 07:00 to around 09:00.

As we dug into new positions, I spotted three FAPLA tanks an AMD, T-34/85, and T-55 crossing the Lomba via the mobile bridge built earlier. 14B panicked and fled; I stopped them via radio. The Ratels, including ZT3 missile variants under Maj Hannes Nortman, responded. The AMD was destroyed by the Ratel 90s, followed by the T-34/85 and T-55. The last missile hit the T-55 dead-on, the turret flew off. One crewman ran, burning, before being gunned down. The Ratel 90s needed multiple HEAT hits, but the ZT3s finished the job. I captured the action with my camera. Suddenly, MiGs returned. Bombs fell in all directions, and two jets fired rockets near KM's eastern flank. A third MiG-21 strafed the area. By 15:00, we returned to 32 Bn's forward HQ to evacuate Absalom and resupply. The Puma helicopter arrived around 22:00. By 01:00, we were driving back in darkness. 14A overheated again and was left behind.

Radio intercepts later confirmed over 300 FAPLA killed, three tanks and a BTR destroyed. On 10 September 1987, 101 Bn, with 901 and 904, effectively shattered most of FAPLA's 21st Brigade largely on their own.

C. Snyman

Concealed Ratel ZT3 during Ops Modular. (H. Nortmann)

Swift missiles (known at the time as the Mongol or ZT3) being loaded into a Ratel ZT3 during Operation Modular. (M. McCallum)

Ratel ZT3s during combat at the Battle of the Lomba River. Note the burning tank in the distance. (M. McCallum)

4

Casspir Mine-Protected Vehicle

The Casspir MPV is widely regarded as the father of modern enclosed V-shaped monocoque hulled mine-resistant ambush protected (MRAP) vehicles, which have since been developed and deployed by many Western armies. The vehicle's design has significantly influenced the development of mine-resistant vehicles worldwide, marking a pivotal moment in military and humanitarian vehicle technology.

The name Casspir was coined by Eddie Caromba in May 1979, derived from an anagram of SAP (South African Police) and CSIR. The Casspir became a symbol of survivability in mine-affected areas due to its innovative design and V-shaped hull, which deflects the explosive force from landmines, making it one of the most effective vehicles of its kind.

Beyond its military applications, the Casspir has also become a key vehicle for demining operations, where it is used to safely remove anti-personnel and anti-tank landmines. Its ruggedness and ability to navigate challenging terrains have also made it the vehicle of choice for various humanitarian and peacekeeping missions, including those conducted by the UN around the world.

Development

In the mid-1970s, the DRU of the CSIR began work on a monocoque hull MPV concept. Simultaneously, the SAP requested a vehicle with specific features: good off-road capability, mine protection, field reparability if a mine was detonated, armour against small arms fire, and the capacity to carry sufficient COIN personnel. These requirements were intended for deployment by SAP-COIN and SWAPOL-COIN units, the latter of which was known as *Koevoet* (crowbar) and operated in northern SWA against the SWAPO insurgents. The Casspir also saw extensive use with 101 Battalion and Romeo Mike "Reaction Force" units.

The SWAPO insurgents would often cross the border into SWA from their bases in Angola to conduct sabotage, intimidation, and assassination raids. Landmines, mostly sourced from Warsaw Pact countries such as the USSR, were frequently used by SWAPO, leading to numerous casualties, particularly among innocent civilians.

The first prototype of the Casspir, named *Flossie*, was delivered by the CSIR in 1978. The initial design was somewhat primitive, with several shortcomings. Made from parts sourced from Bedford trucks, it featured a V-bottom armoured monocoque hull with suspension modules located externally to allow for easier repair and replacement if blown off by a mine. However, the Unimog 352 engine initially intended for the vehicle proved unsuitable. To improve the design, the UCCD (the largest importer of Mercedes-Benz parts in South Africa) was approached for assistance. This led to the successful installation of a Mercedes-Benz LA1113/42 driveline, including the OM352 engine, axles, gearbox, and transfer box.

Casspir MK3 at Armed Forces Day 2023. (C. Hugo)

Eland 90 Armoured Car in Dark Earth scheme. (Artwork by David Bocquelet)

Eland 90 Mk7 specifications			
Crew	3	Gradient (%)	42
Combat weight (t)	6	Trench (m)	0.5
Power-to-weight ratio (hp/t)	14.5	Engine power output (hp)	87
Length (m)	4.04	Number of forward gears	6
Width (m)	2.01	Number of reverse gears	1
Height (m)	2.5	Main weapon calibre (mm)	90
Max. road speed (km/h)	90	Auxiliary gun calibre (mm) x2	7.62
Fuel capacity (ℓ)	142	Ammunition of main weapon	29
Max. road range (km)	450	Ammunition of the auxiliary gun	3,800

Eland 60 Armoured Car in Dark Earth scheme. (Artwork by David Bocquelet)

Eland 60 specifications			
Crew	3	Gradient (%)	42
Combat weight (t)	5.32	Trench (m)	0.5
Power-to-weight ratio (hp/t)	16.4	Engine power output (hp)	87
Length (m)	4.04	Number of forward gears	6
Width (m)	2.01	Number of reverse gears	1
Height (m)	1.88	Main weapon calibre (mm)	60
Max. road speed (km/h)	90	Auxiliary gun calibre (mm) x2	7.62
Fuel capacity (ℓ)	142	Ammunition of main weapon	56
Max. road range (km)	450	Ammunition of the auxiliary gun	2,400

Buffel Mine Protected Vehicle in Dark Earth scheme. (Artwork by David Bocquelet)

Buffel specifications			
Crew	1+10	Gradient (%)	60
Combat weight (t)	6.1	Trench (m)	1.2
Power-to-weight ratio (hp/t)	20.4	Engine power output (hp)	125
Length (m)	5.10	Number of forward gears	8
Width (m)	2.05	Number of reverse gears	4
Height (m)	2.96	Main weapon calibre (mm) x2	7.62
Max. road speed (km/h)	96	Auxiliary gun calibre (mm)	-
Fuel capacity (ℓ)	200	Ammunition of main weapon	1,000
Max. road range (km)	1,000	Ammunition of the auxiliary gun	-

Moffel. (Artwork by David Bocquelet)

Ratel 12.7 in Dark Earth scheme. (Artwork by David Bocquelet)

Ratel 12.7 specifications			
Crew	3 + 6	Gradient (%)	60
Combat weight (t)	18.9	Trench (m)	1.15
Power-to-weight ratio (hp/t)	14.9	Engine power output (hp)	282
Length (m)	7.2	Number of forward gears	6
Width (m)	2.7	Number of reverse gears	2
Height (m)	2.89	Main weapon calibre (mm)	12.7
Max. road speed (km/h)	105	Auxiliary gun calibre (mm) x 2	7.62
Fuel capacity (ℓ)	480	Ammunition of main weapon	300
Max. road range (km)	1,000	Ammunition of the auxiliary gun	3,000

Ratel 12.7 in the three colour scheme introduced in the early 2020s. (Artwork by David Bocquelet)

Ratel 20 in Dark Earth scheme. (Artwork by David Bocquelet)

Ratel 20 specifications			
Crew	3 + 8–11	Gradient (%)	60
Combat weight (t)	18.9	Trench (m)	1.15
Power-to-weight ratio (hp/t)	14.9	Engine power output (hp)	282
Length (m)	7.2	Number of forward gears	6
Width (m)	2.70	Number of reverse gears	2
Height (m)	2.94	Main weapon calibre (mm)	20
Max. road speed (km/h)	105	Auxiliary gun calibre (mm) x 2	7.62
Fuel capacity	480	Ammunition of main weapon	1,200
Max. road range (km)	1,000	Ammunition of the auxiliary gun	6,000

Ratel 20 in the three colour scheme introduced in the 1990s. (Artwork by David Bocquelet)

Ratel 60 in Dark Earth scheme. (Artwork by David Bocquelet)

Ratel 60 specifications			
Crew	3+7	Gradient (%)	60
Combat weight (t)	18.9	Trench (m)	1.15
Power-to-weight ratio (hp/t)	14.9	Engine power output (hp)	282
Length (m)	7.2	Number of forward gears	6
Width (m)	2.7	Number of reverse gears	2
Height (m)	2.89	Main weapon calibre (mm)	60
Max. road speed (km/h)	105	Auxiliary gun calibre (mm) x 2	7.62
Fuel capacity (ℓ)	480	Ammunition of main weapon	45
Max. road range (km)	1,000	Ammunition of the auxiliary gun	6,000

Ratel 60 in the three colour scheme introduced in the 1990s. (Artwork by David Bocquelet)

Ratel 90 in Dark Earth scheme. (Artwork by David Bocquelet)

Ratel 90 Specifications			
Crew	3+6	Gradient (%)	60
Combat weight (t)	20	Trench (m)	1.15
Power-to-weight ratio (hp/t)	14.1	Engine power output (hp)	282
Length (m)	7.2	Number of forward gears	6
Width (m)	2.7	Number of reverse gears	2
Height (m)	2.92	Main weapon calibre (mm)	90
Max. road speed (km/h)	105	Auxiliary gun calibre (mm) x 2	7.62
Fuel capacity (ℓ)	480	Ammunition of main weapon	50
Max. road range (km)	1,000	Ammunition of the auxiliary gun	6,000

Ratel 90 in the three colour scheme introduced in the 1990s. (Artwork by David Bocquelet)

Ratel 81 in Dark Earth scheme. (Artwork by David Bocquelet)

Ratel 81 specifications			
Crew	2+3	Gradient (%)	60
Combat weight (t)	16.7	Trench (m)	1.15
Power-to-weight ratio (hp/t)	16.8	Engine power output (hp)	282
Length (m)	7.2	Number of forward gears	6
Width (m)	2.7	Number of reverse gears	2
Height (m)	2.5	Main weapon calibre (mm)	81
Max. road speed (km/h)	105	Auxiliary gun calibre (mm)	7.62
Fuel capacity (ℓ)	480	Ammunition of main weapon	148
Max. road range (km)	1,000	Ammunition of the auxiliary gun	1,200

Ratel 81 in the three colour scheme introduced in the 1990s. (Artwork by David Bocquelet)

Ratel ZT-3 in Dark Earth scheme. (Artwork by David Bocquelet)

Ratel ZT3 specifications			
Crew	4	Gradient (%)	60
Combat weight (t)	19.2	Trench (m)	1.15
Power-to-weight ratio (hp/t)	14.8	Engine power output (hp)	282
Length (m)	7.2	Number of forward gears	6
Width (m)	2.7	Number of reverse gears	2
Height (m)	3.34	Main weapon calibre (mm) x 2	127
Max. road speed (km/h)	105	Auxiliary gun calibre (mm)	7.62
Fuel capacity (ℓ)	480	Ammunition of main weapon	12
Max. road range (km)	1,000	Ammunition of the auxiliary gun	1,200

Ratel ZT-3 in the three colour scheme introduced in the 1990s. (Artwork by David Bocquelet)

Casspir in Dark Earth scheme. (Artwork by David Bocquelet)

Casspir specifications			
Crew	2+12	Gradient (%)	50
Combat weight (t)	10.7	Trench (m)	1
Power-to-weight ratio (hp/t)	15.5	Engine power output (hp)	166
Length (m)	6.9	Number of forward gears	5
Width (m)	2.5	Number of reverse gears	1
Height (m)	3.1	Main weapon calibre (mm)	12.7
Max. road speed (km/h)	90	Auxiliary gun calibre (mm)	-
Fuel capacity (ℓ)	200	Ammunition of main weapon	Unkown
Max. road range (km)	800	Ammunition of the auxiliary gun	-

Casspir in the three colour scheme introduced in the 1990s. (Artwork by David Bocquelet)

G6 Rhino Self-Propelled Howitzer Vehicle in Dark Earth scheme. (Artwork by David Bocquelet)

G6-45 specifications			
Crew	6	Gradient (%)	40
Combat weight (t)	46	Trench (m)	1
Power-to-weight ratio (hp/t)	12	Engine power output (hp)	550
Length (m)	9.2	Number of forward gears	6
Width (m)	3.5	Number of reverse gears	1
Height (m)	3.4	Main weapon calibre (mm)	155
Max. road speed (km/h)	85	Auxiliary gun calibre (mm)	7.62
Fuel capacity (ℓ)	700	Ammunition of main weapon	39
Max. road range (km)	700	Ammunition of the auxiliary gun	2,000

G6 Rhino Self-Propelled Howitzer Vehicle in the three colour scheme introduced in the 1990s. (Artwork by David Bocquelet)

Ystervark Self-Propelled Anti-Aircraft Gun deployed for action with side shields down. (Artwork by David Bocquelet)

Ystervark Self-Propelled Anti-Aircraft Gun ready to move with side shields up. (Artwork by David Bocquelet)

Ystervark specifications			
Crew	3	Gradient (%)	60
Combat weight (t)	7.7	Trench (m)	0.5
Power-to-weight ratio (hp/t)	20.4	Engine power output (hp)	124
Length (m)	5.1	Number of forward gears	4
Width (m)	2.05	Number of reverse gears	1
Height (m)	2.96	Main weapon calibre (mm)	20
Max. road speed (km/h)	90	Auxiliary gun calibre (mm)	-
Fuel capacity (ℓ)	200	Ammunition of main weapon	675
Max. road range (km)	950	Ammunition of the auxiliary gun	-

Bateleur Multiple Rocket Launcher. (Artwork by David Bocquelet)

Bateleur specifications			
Crew	5	Gradient (%)	70
Combat weight (t)	21.5	Trench (m)	0.5
Power-to-weight ratio (hp/t)	12.5	Engine power output (hp)	268
Length (m)	8.53	Number of forward gears	8
Width (m)	2.45	Number of reverse gears	1
Height (m)	3.12	Main weapon calibre (mm)	127
Max. road speed (km/h)	90	Auxiliary gun calibre (mm)	7.62
Fuel capacity (ℓ)	400	Ammunition of main weapon	40
Max. road range (km)	600	Ammunition of the auxiliary gun	1,000

Olifant Mk1A Main Battle Tank in Dark Earth scheme. (Artwork by David Bocquelet)

Olifant Mk1A specifications			
Crew	4	Gradient (%)	58
Combat weight (t)	56	Trench (m)	3.45
Power-to-weight ratio (hp/t)	13.39	Engine power output (hp)	750
Length (m)	7.56	Number of forward gears	2
Width (m)	3.39	Number of reverse gears	1
Height (m)	2.94	Main weapon calibre (mm)	105
Max. road speed (km/h)	45	Auxiliary gun calibre (mm)	7.62
Fuel capacity (ℓ)	1240	Ammunition of main weapon	72
Max. road range (km)	350	Ammunition of the auxiliary gun	5,600

Olifant Mk1A Main Battle Tank in the three colour scheme introduced in the 1990s. (Artwork by David Bocquelet)

By May 1979, the first prototype was ready for trial. Following a brief trial period, the SAP accepted the design and placed an order for 140 vehicles in early 1980. Ultimately, 190 Casspir Mk1 vehicles were manufactured by Henred Fruehauf.

Design Features

The Casspir was designed primarily as a mine-resistant APC which could operate in some of the most hostile terrains in the world. The Casspir has several characteristics which have led to its success. It is of 4x4 design coupled with differential lock, making use of four large run-flat tyres which are designed to resist the effects of deflation when punctured. It has a high ground clearance of 365mm (14.4in) which, coupled with the all-important V-shaped armoured underbelly, helps disperse and deflect mine blast energy away from the hull. Making use of commercially available parts reduces its reliance on a specialised logistical train (the process of producing and supplying parts) with the added benefit of decreasing the need for support vehicles for spare parts and specialised maintenance while deployed. The front of the vehicle is strengthened and optimised for bundu bashing. It can travel long distances on-road, 800km (500mi) without having to refuel and at a comfortable pace of 90km/h (56mph), which arguably makes it one of the most versatile APCs ever fielded. The Casspir Mk3 (and subsequent variants) used by the SADF has a thicker V-shaped hull, 14:00x20 tyres and a different engine. The Casspir Mk3 standard also includes structural alterations for improved mobility, with more robust axles.

In 1981, the production of the Casspir APC was transferred to TFM Limited, which designed the Casspir Mk2. Externally, the Casspir Mk2 closely resembled the Casspir Mk1, but with notable modifications, including the removal of the escape hatch on the left side of the vehicle. TFM Limited also developed a range of support vehicles based on the Casspir APC hull in 1982.

Impressed by the Casspir's success in counterinsurgency operations against SWAPO, the SADF took an interest in the Casspir as early as 1982/83. The SADF incorporated the Casspir Mk2 and Casspir Mk3 versions into the South West Africa Territorial Force (SWATF) 101 Battalion and the elite 5 Recces.

Over the course of 25 years, the ownership of the Casspir production companies changed hands multiple times. TFM was taken over by Reumech. Reumech was later acquired by Vickers Defence Systems (UK), and subsequently renamed Vickers OMC. When Alvis (a UK defence company) purchased Vickers Defence Systems and formed Alvis Vickers, Vickers OMC became Alvis OMC. In 2004, BAE Systems acquired Alvis Vickers, and Alvis OMC was renamed Land Systems OMC. In 2015, Denel, a South African defence firm, purchased a 75% controlling share in Land Systems OMC, returning ownership of the Casspir to South Africa. In 2007, 167 Casspirs were upgraded under Project Gijima. Over the years, newer hull designs such as the NG2000 and NG2000B have emerged. As of 2017, more than 2,800 Casspirs in various configurations have been produced for both South African and export markets.

Despite the shift to newer vehicles, it is estimated that 170 Casspirs are still in service with the SANDF. Foreign users of the Casspir include countries such as Angola, Benin, Burundi, Democratic Republic of the Congo, Djibouti, Egypt, Ghana, India, Indonesia, Iraq, Malawi, Mozambique, Namibia, Nepal, Peru, Saudi Arabia, Senegal, Sierra Leone, Tanzania, Uganda, and even the United States.

Mobility

The Casspir features a 4x4 configuration, specifically designed for the challenging conditions of the African battlespace. Its design is characterised by versatility and exceptional cross-country capability, making it well-suited for rugged and varied terrains. Unlike tracked vehicles, the Casspir requires less maintenance, making it a more efficient option for long-term operations in the field.

With a ground clearance of 365mm (14.4in), the Casspir can ford up to 1m (3.3ft) of water, ensuring it can traverse various obstacles. The Casspir Mk2 variant is powered by the ADE 352T six-cylinder turbocharged diesel engine, producing 166hp (124kW) and a power-to-weight ratio of 15.5hp/t. The engine is positioned at the front of the vehicle, coupled to a Mercedes-Benz MB G5 five-speed synchromesh manual transmission. This setup offers five forward gears and one reverse, providing flexibility in various operational scenarios. The vehicle's power is transmitted through a Mercedes-Benz VG 500-3W transfer box to the axles. The Casspir Mk1 and Mk2 use Mercedes-Benz axles, while the Mk3 is equipped with ZF axles. The rear axle is fitted with a differential lock for enhanced traction on difficult terrain.

The Casspir Mk2C (I) variant, introduced in 2010, features an upgraded driveline system developed by Denel Mechem. The power pack in this variant consists of a Tata 697 TC diesel engine, which produces 157hp (117kW) at 2,800rpm, coupled to a Tata GBS-50 transmission with five forward gears and one reverse. The Tata transfer case ensures effective distribution of power. The front axles are Tata FA 106, rated for 6,500kg, while the rear axles, Tata RA 106, are rated for 10t.

The Casspir's suspension system is one of its standout features, specifically designed for the demands of the African bush. The vehicle is highly stable, offering excellent off-road mobility. Its semi-elliptic leaf spring suspension (front and rear) provides significant deflection, allowing the vehicle to absorb shock from rough terrain. To enhance stability and ride comfort, check straps were added to counter axle rebound, ensuring a smoother experience on uneven surfaces.

Endurance and logistics

The Casspir is equipped with a 200ℓ (52.8gal) fuel tank, providing it with an operational range of 800km (500mi) on-road and 400km (250mi) off-road. Its road speed reaches 90km/h (56mph), while its cross-country speed is around 28km/h (17mph), allowing for reliable movement across various terrains. The vehicle's modular design was specifically chosen to simplify maintenance and reduce logistical demands. This design allows for easy access to interchangeable components, ensuring that repairs can be conducted quickly and with minimal effort. The Casspir also features a 200/220ℓ (52.8/58gal) water tank, providing essential water supplies for extended operations, especially under the harsh conditions it often encounters in the field.

Main armament

While the Casspir MPV does not come with standard weapons, a primary gun mount is sometimes installed above the driver's compartment to increase its defensive capabilities. The armament typically consists of either a set of dual 7.62mm BMGs or Browning M2 12.7mm (.50 calibre), depending on operational requirements. During the South African Border War, some Casspirs were retrofitted with 20mm Hispano cannons, originally from retired South African Air Force (SAAF) fighter planes, such as the Spitfire Mk.IX and DE Havilland Vampire jets.

In addition, units like Koevoet made use of captured weapons, including the KPV/KPVT 14.5mm heavy machine gun, further enhancing the vehicle's firepower. The co-driver's front window can also be fitted with a machine gun mounted on a gimbal, allowing for improved versatility in close combat. For additional close-in defence, the Casspir is equipped with six gun ports on each side of the troop compartment, as well as two in the rear doors, ensuring that personnel can engage threats from multiple angles if necessary.

Vehicle layout

The Casspir features a robust vehicle layout, with both the engine and transmission housed inside the armoured hull to minimise damage in the event of a mine detonation. The vehicle has a crew of two a driver and a vehicle commander /gunner and can accommodate 10–12 passengers. The Casspir follows a traditional vehicle design, with the engine positioned at the front, the crew compartment located directly behind it, and the troop compartment extending to the rear of the vehicle.

The troop compartment is equipped with three rectangular bulletproof windows and six firing ports on each side of the hull, providing defensive fire capabilities for passengers. The passenger seats face inward and are fitted with four-point safety harnesses to ensure occupant safety during operations.

Access to the troop compartment is facilitated via two air-operated rear doors, which can be remotely operated by the driver. These doors are reinforced with bulletproof window blocks, enhancing the vehicle's protection. The crew compartment roof is designed as an open top, extending from just behind the driver and commander to the rear of the vehicle. During the South African Border War, the roof hatches in both the crew and troop compartments were often left open, especially during the hot summer months, to allow for ventilation. Early versions of the Casspir featured a small fan, retrofitted to keep onboard equipment cool. In modern variants, air-conditioning units are commonly fitted to improve comfort and maintain optimal operating conditions.

Casspir MK3. Driver station. AAD 2024. (D. Venter)

Casspir MK3. AAD 2022. (D. Venter)

Casspir MK3. Troop compartment. AAD 2024. (D. Venter)

Protection

The Casspir's protection system is one of its defining features, ensuring the safety of its occupants in hostile environments. The vehicle is capable of withstanding a triple TM-57 mine blast equivalent to 21kg (41lbs) of TNT under any of its wheels or a double mine blast under the hull. The Casspir's success as an MPV lies in its narrow V-bottom armoured monocoque hull, which effectively deflects blast energy and debris, directing it away from the hull and thus minimising damage to the vehicle and its occupants.

The fuel tank is equipped with a blast-proof cap and is positioned inside the armoured hull, offering further protection against mine blasts and reducing the risk of secondary explosions. The vehicle's hull is also rated to protect against 7.62×51mm NATO and 7.62×39mm AK-47 ball ammunition, ensuring the crew and passengers remain safe from small arms fire and shrapnel in combat situations.

The Casspir Family

The versatility of the Casspir APC hull is best appreciated when considering the extensive range of combat and support vehicles that have been developed based on this platform. South African Motorised Infantry forces utilise various Casspir-based vehicles, primarily built on the Mk2 and Mk3 hulls. These variants are adapted for a range of operational roles and include: 81mm Mortar Weapons Platform, 106mm Recoilless Rifle Weapons Platform, Artillery Fire Control, Electronic Warfare, Blesbok Cargo Support, Duiker Fuel Bowser, Gemsbok Recovery Vehicle, Plofadder Mine-Clearing Vehicle, Ambulance, Vehicle-Mounted Metal Detection System, Groundshout Psychological Warfare System and Law Enforcement.

81mm Mortar Weapons Platform

The 81mm Mortar Weapons Platform is based on the Casspir Mk3 and involves a rebuild of an existing vehicle. It features a fully enclosed crew compartment at the front and a mortar compartment at the rear, offering armoured protection on all sides. Bulletproof windows are installed on the sides and rear for improved visibility during operations.

Casspir 81mm Mortar Weapons Platform. (J. Van Zyl)

The platform carries 192 mortar rounds, stored in ready-to-use racks along with the required charges and fuses. By integrating the 81mm mortar with the Casspir, the time taken to move in and out of action is reduced, enabling quicker target engagement and minimising the risk of the vehicle being located and neutralised by counter-battery fire.

Additionally, the mortar can be removed and deployed for use in the ground role if needed or if the vehicle becomes disabled. A 7.62mm machine gun is mounted on the roof for all-round defence.

106mm Recoilless Rifle Weapons Platform

The 106mm Recoilless Rifle Weapons Platform, also based on the Casspir Mk3 and rebuilt from an existing vehicle, features a fully enclosed crew and troop compartment, with the 106mm M40 recoilless rifle mounted at the rear. The side and rear panels can be folded down, allowing the gun to be laid on target.

This platform carries a total of 12 ready-to-use 105mm HEAT rounds, each capable of penetrating 450mm (17.72in) of RHA and being used accurately at a range of 1.1km (0.68mi). Like the 81mm mortar platform, the gun can be removed and used in the ground role if needed, or if the vehicle is disabled. A 7.62mm BMG is also mounted on the roof for all-round defence. There are currently 32 of these platforms in operational service with the SANDF.

Artillery Fire Control

The SANDF operates several artillery fire control vehicles based on the Casspir platform. These vehicles are easily distinguishable by their additional radio antennas and a large telescopic mast, which are used for target acquisition and coordination during artillery operations. Details on the specific numbers and capabilities of these vehicles are not widely available.

Electronic warfare

Several Casspir Mk3 vehicles were converted by the SANDF for EW use. Specific details regarding the numbers and capabilities of these vehicles are not publicly available. However, they are understood to have been adapted for operations involving signals intelligence, jamming, and other forms of electronic warfare to support the SADF's operational needs during the South African Border War and beyond.

Blesbok Cargo Support Vehicle

The Blesbok was a dedicated logistics vehicle used by COIN units during the South African Border War. It was typically allocated to fighting groups of four Casspir APCs, where it would carry ammunition, rations, spare parts, fuel, and camping equipment, allowing the groups to operate independently for up to a week without resupply. The Blesbok features an armoured two-man driving cab at the front, with individual doors for the driver and commander. The cargo area at the rear is equipped with drop sides for easy loading and offloading and has a five-ton capacity. It can also be fitted with a 1,000ℓ (264gal) fuel or water tank. A 7.62mm BMG can be mounted on the roof and in the front left window. A total of 160 vehicles were built for the SAP.

Duiker Fuel Bowser

The Duiker is a dedicated diesel fuel bowser built on the Casspir Mk3 hull. It features an armoured two-man driving cab at the front, with individual doors for the driver and commander, and a 3,000ℓ or 5,000ℓ (792gal or 1,320gal) fuel tank at the rear. The fuel system uses a gravity feed with an optional electric pump. A 5.56mm Vector Mini-SS light machine gun is mounted on the roof and the front left window for defence. A total of 30 vehicles were built for the SAP.

Casspir 106mm Recoilless Rifle Weapons Platform. Armed Forces Day 2019. (J. Van Zyl)

Blesbok Cargo Support Vehicle. Sandstone Heritage Estate. D. Venter

Duiker Fuel Bowser.
Sandstone Heritage Estate.
(D. Venter)

Gemsbok Recovery Vehicle

The Gemsbok is a 15-ton recovery vehicle based on the Casspir Mk3 hull. It features an extended armoured five-man crew cab with individual doors for the driver and commander, and an additional side door on the left-hand side. The recovery equipment is located at the rear, and the vehicle weighs 15.8t. Thirty Gemsbok vehicles were produced for the SAP.

Plofadder Mine-Clearing Vehicle

The Plofadder is a dedicated mine-clearing vehicle based on the Casspir. It features an armoured two-man driving cab and uses a 160AT rocket-propelled mine-clearing system, which is loaded into the back of the Casspir on rails and launched through the open roof. The rails for loading the containers are carried on the side of the vehicle, and the cable drum for the remote control system is located on the right side of the vehicle.

Ambulance

The Casspir Ambulance is a modified Casspir MPV with an armoured two-man driving cab at the front. The rear passenger compartment is modified to carry two stretcher cases and three seats. The vehicle is equipped with standard medical equipment storage, including racks for drips. Blackout curtains are fitted in the rear compartment to maintain operational security in the field.

Mechem Vehicle-Mounted Metal Detection System

The MV MM DS was developed by Denel Mechem and is based on a modified Casspir. The vehicle tows a rubber mat containing the Vehicle Array Mine Detection System (VAMIDS) system, which detects and marks the location of landmines using white marking fluid. This system has been successfully deployed in countries like Sudan and Eritrea for mine clearance operations.

Groundshout psychological warfare system

The Groundshout system was used for psychological warfare and was assigned to 101 Battalion in 1987. It featured 32 speakers driven by 4,900-watt AEM amps and was capable of broadcasting messages and sounds up to 8km (5mi). Mounted on a hydraulic telescopic boom, the speakers could be elevated and directed for maximum effect. The system was used to broadcast screaming animal sounds and armoured vehicle noises to disturb enemy morale. It was reported that FAPLA troops in the Lomba trenches were particularly disturbed by the system. Groundshout vehicles have also been used by the SANDF for communication during the COVID-19 pandemic.

Law enforcement

Following the first democratic elections in 1994, the SAP was renamed the South African Police Service (SAPS). With less need for the Casspir, the SAPS sold a large number of the vehicles. The remaining Casspirs were allocated to public order police units specialising in riot control. These vehicles were modified with larger bulletproof windows for increased visibility in urban areas and grills to protect against rocks. An innovative feature includes a front buffer (bulbar) that can be lowered from inside the vehicle to clear barricades and other obstructions. A wire cutter can also be mounted on the roof.

Sesspir

The Sesspir was a six-wheel variant of the Casspir (hence the name *Sesspir*, six in Afrikaans), developed for trials in 1984–85 in response to feedback from SADF troops. The Sesspir featured an extended nose to accommodate additional front wheels to prevent immobilisation in the event of a mine detonation. However, the additional wheels placed excessive demand on the Casspir's standard engine, leading to poor performance. After operational trials, one of the two Sesspir vehicles was destroyed during Operation Firewood, and the other was converted back to a standard Casspir.

Plofadder. (Open source)

Sesspir. (Open source)

NG2000

Building upon the success of the Casspir, Denel Mechem introduced a new generation of the vehicle, originally designated Mk4 and later rebranded as the Casspir NG2000 series. This new model incorporates advanced production techniques and improvements over the original design, ensuring that the Casspir NG2000 continues to meet modern operational needs.

Powered by a WEICHAI WD10.290E32 six-cylinder inline diesel engine, the vehicle produces 290hp (213kW) at 2,200rpm, delivering a power-to-weight ratio of 14.6kW/t. The engine is water-cooled and uses EURO 2-compliant diesel injection. The transmission system comprises a ZF Series gearbox coupled with a ZF VG Series transfer case, enabling a 4x4 drivetrain with nine forward and one reverse gear.

The Casspir NG2000 Ambulance is equipped with semi-elliptic leaf spring suspension and double heavy-duty dual-acting shock absorbers on both axles, enhancing off-road mobility and ride comfort even under load. Tyres are 14.00 x R20 steel-belted run-flats with integrated flat devices for sustained mobility in the event of punctures or blast damage. The vehicle features hydraulically

NG2000 Ambulance variant. AAD 2018. (D. Venter)

assisted steering and a fully hydraulic foot brake system, while the parking brake is controlled by a spring brake cylinder. An anti-lock braking system (ABS) comes standard.

Electrically, the vehicle runs a 24-volt system supported by two 12V batteries and a 120A/h alternator. With a length of 7.38m (290in), a width of 2.6m (103in), a height of 3.02m (119in) excluding spare wheels, and a ground clearance of 430mm (16.93in), the ambulance maintains a substantial profile yet remains highly mobile. Its gross vehicle mass is 14,050kg (31,963lbs). Operational performance includes a safe road speed of 80km/h (50mph) and a maximum top speed of 110km/h (68mph), depending on terrain. It has an impressive road range of 600–850km (373–528mi), supported by a 400ℓ (106gal) fuel tank. Unlike some other variants, the ambulance version is not amphibious.

Internally, the vehicle can accommodate a driver, co-driver, four sitting wounded passengers, and four stretcher-bound casualties, making it well-suited for high-casualty scenarios in conflict zones. Standard equipment includes a basic operator's tool kit and front-mounted tool storage, with optional upgrades such as automatic transmission and enhanced run-flat wheels available.

Operational History

During the South African Border War, Casspirs operated by Koevoet would travel in fighting groups of four, accompanied by a Blesbok (supply/logistics vehicle) and a Duiker (diesel/fuel bowser). These convoys would cover 600–800km (373–497mi) over five to seven days, with each Casspir carrying essential supplies and provisions for the mission. Each vehicle was equipped with a 200ℓ (53gal) water tank and two spare tires, mounted on either side of the lower exterior hull or on either side of the rear troop compartment.

Since its introduction in 1984, the Casspir family of APCs has played an essential role in motorised operations with the former SADF during the South African Border War. It was especially significant for the motorised infantry of 101 Battalion, a quick-reaction unit stationed in northern SWA, just south of the Angolan border. Using the Casspir's mobility and speed, 101 Battalion was able to quickly respond to SWAPO insurgency raids crossing from Angola into SWA.

Each company within 101 Battalion typically operated in teams of four Casspirs, equipped with two Hispano-Suiza 20mm cannons, six 12.7mm BMGs, four 7.62mm BMGs, and four 60mm patrol mortars. Bushman trackers, known for their exceptional skills in tracking, would follow the insurgent *spoor* (tracks), while the Casspirs, carrying heavy armament, would trail behind, ready to provide overwhelming fire support once contact with the insurgents was made. The combination of speed, mobility, and firepower made the Casspir incredibly effective in these operations.

On average, 101 Battalion engaged in 200 contacts per year with insurgent groups numbering between five and 200 members. However, following the independence of Namibia in 1991, 101 Battalion was disbanded, and the Casspir continued its service in other missions.

Casspirs were deployed during the 1998 SADC intervention in Lesotho, where they played a crucial role as part of the SANDF's efforts. The Casspir has since become a symbol of UN peacekeeping forces in mine-riddled conflict zones across Africa, offering protection to both soldiers and civilians in unstable environments. Exported Casspirs have seen extensive service in the Middle East, particularly in Iraq and Afghanistan, where they have been credited with saving countless coalition soldiers' lives by offering protection against landmines and small arms fire.

The role of Casspirs in COIN operations during the South African Border War is well-documented in Peter Stiff's book *Taming the Landmine.*

Mine incidents

The Casspir's primary role was in counterinsurgency while protecting its users from landmine blasts. Table 2 shows its success in this regard.

Conclusion

The Casspir stands as the first monocoque hull APC to enter military service during the Cold War and is widely regarded by military analysts as the progenitor of all subsequent MPVs. Its design set the standard for modern MPVs and influenced the development of MRAP vehicles fielded by the United States and most Western nations. For its time, the Casspir was one of the best MPVs in the world, offering an unprecedented combination of protection, mobility, and versatility.

The Casspir's legacy spans 35 years, with continuous research and modifications ensuring that it remains a defining benchmark against which other wheeled MPVs are measured. It became the backbone of the SADF motorised battalions, playing a vital role throughout the 23 years of the South African Border War. Despite the absence of production of new Casspirs for the SANDF since 1993/94, the Casspir family continues to serve in various capacities.

In 2004, an extensive rebuilding programme was launched as part of Project Gijima, which refurbished 174 Casspir Mk2 vehicles, upgrading them to the Casspir Mk3 standard by 2007. Today, an estimated 370 Casspirs remain in service, primarily assigned to the SANDF's motorised infantry battalions. At present, no immediate replacement for the Casspir is planned within the SANDF.

Table 2: Certified Casspir mine incidents

Type of mine	Incidents	Killed	Injured	Personnel
Single mines (6kg [13lbs] TNT)	191	6	167	-
Double mines (12kg [26lbs] TNT)	35	2	69	-
Triple mines (18kg [39lbs] TNT)	1	1	0	-
Four mines (24kg [52lbs] TNT)	2	3	16	-
Total number	229	12	252	2,784
Total percentage		0.004%	0.09%	

5

G6 Rhino Self-Propelled Howitzer Vehicle

Developed during the height of the Cold War, the G6 Rhino was designed by South Africa to replace its ageing Second World War artillery pieces, allowing the country to counter the Eastern Bloc-supplied artillery used by the MPLA and FAPLA. It is a three-axle, six-wheeled self-propelled howitzer vehicle, designed to deliver powerful long-range strikes, while also boasting significant mobility. Today, the G6 Rhino forms the backbone of the SANDF's artillery arm, with a total of 43 vehicles fielded by the South African forces.

Development

During the 1960s and 1970s, the SADF still relied on Second World War-era artillery, such as the 88mm QF gun (G1), the 140mm cannon (G2), and the Sexton self-propelled artillery, among others. By the late 1960s, it became clear that these outdated systems would need to be replaced to maintain a modern and capable artillery force. In 1968, artillery gunners set forth the requirements to modernise their arsenal, and this was formally established in 1973.

South Africa had also acquired several American-made M1 155mm towed howitzers, designated as G3, which were instrumental in developing gun drills, doctrine, and logistics for a new artillery system. This new system would eventually be realised in the form of the G5-45 155mm advanced long-range field artillery system, often referred to as the Leopard. The project to develop this advanced system began in 1976 under Project Sherbet III, led by the Space Research Corporation (SRC) and its famous director, Dr. Gerald Bull.

The contract to design the G6's hull and drivetrain was awarded to Sandock-Austral, whose design team handled the bulk of the work. Meanwhile, LEW was tasked with designing the turret and gun control system, while the G5-45's integration into a turret was assigned to Kentron. Electronics System Development (ESD) developed the rammer control system for loading, and Naschem took responsibility for the ammunition subsystems. The result was the G6-45, equipped with the same 155mm gun as the G5-45.

The formal development of the G6 self-propelled gun-howitzer began in 1979 at ARMSCOR under Project Zenula. The first advanced prototype was completed in October 1981, and by 1987, four G6 vehicles had been built. These prototypes were pressed into service during the South African Border War that same year. One of the vehicles experienced an engine failure due to a bolt accidentally falling into the compressor during a maintenance change, but a replacement engine was flown in, and the G6 returned to action after repairs. By mid-December 1987, all four G6 vehicles successfully returned to South Africa under their own power.

Full-scale production of the G6 began in 1988 and continued until 1994. A modernisation program, codenamed Project Vasvat, was implemented in 1993 to ensure that all G6 vehicles had uniform equipment and capabilities. Variants of the G6, known as the H45, are currently operated by Oman (24 units) and the United Arab Emirates (78 units).

Denel Land Systems has continued to develop and upgrade the G6 platform, unveiling the G6-52 in 2003. This model featured significant improvements in mobility, speed, range, accuracy, ease of operation, rate of fire, and protection against counter-battery fire.

G6 prototype. Kerkstraat Pretoria 1983. (W. Williams)

Two variants of the G6-52 were produced: one with a standard 23ℓ chamber and the other with a larger 25ℓ chamber, known as the ER (extended range) designation.

As of this writing, 15 G6-45s are undergoing an obsolescence upgrade under Project Muhali, aimed at replacing outdated components. Originally set for completion by June 2021 at a cost of R144 million, the project faced significant delays due to challenges at Denel, pushing the completion date to 14 March 2024. Additionally, Project Topstar was scheduled for completion on 15 March 2024, focusing on upgrading the gun-laying and navigation systems of the G6-45, further enhancing the vehicle's modern operational capabilities.

Design Features

The G6 sports a low-silhouetted 6x6 wheeled hull designed and optimised for the distances and terrain it would operate in, which can be described as some of the most hostile in the world. The G6 is characterised by its six massive 21:00x25 wheels, fast setup time, bush-breaking ability and versatility as a howitzer platform. In skilled hands, during the South African Border War, the G6 proved itself more than capable of inflicting heavy losses. The G5 was designed with a secondary self-defensive direct anti-tank role in mind. It is thought that it can defeat any composite armoured MBT of the time. The same is true for the G6. It came as a nasty surprise to FAPLA, as it dominated the battlespace by outshooting, outranging and outmanoeuvring enemy artillery.

Mobility

The long distances and low force density typical of Southern Africa's battlefields necessitated a vehicle that could travel independently.

The G6's wheeled configuration grants it significant operational mobility, eliminating the need for heavy transport or rail to reach its destination. This feature aligns with the SADF's doctrine of mobile warfare, which emphasises speed and flexibility.

The G6 is equipped with a central tyre-inflation system that adjusts tyre pressure for soft, medium, or hard terrain while on the move, enabling it to adapt to different conditions seamlessly. All six wheels are fitted with hydro-pneumatic drum brakes, and the vehicle can continue to operate even if one of the rear or middle wheels is lost.

Despite these advantages, the G6's wheeled configuration comes with trade-offs. Achieving acceptable cross-country mobility for vehicles over 10t requires a larger overall size and increased mechanical complexity compared to tracked vehicles.

The Magirus Deutz BF12L513 FC V12 air-cooled diesel engine powers the G6, generating 550hp (410kW), allowing it to accelerate from 0–30km/h (0–19mph) in 12 seconds. The engine and gearbox are mounted on a subframe located between the driver's and fighting compartments, maximising internal space and protection.

The Denel Vehicle Systems automatic gearbox (part of the RENK family of gearboxes) provides six forward gears and one reverse. If necessary, the gearbox can be overridden manually. The vehicle operates with a permanent six-wheel drive configuration, which includes selectable longitudinal and differential locks, offering excellent mobility across diverse terrain. Torsion bar suspension units and hydraulic shock dampers are present on all six wheels, with hydraulically assisted steering enhancing manoeuvrability.

The G6's turret houses a Deutz F2L511 air-cooled two-cylinder four-stroke diesel engine, producing 45hp (34kW) to power the vehicle's batteries and air-conditioning units for crew comfort. The G6-52 variant features an upgraded 50hp (37kW) turret-mounted auxiliary power unit (APU) engine.

The vehicle's electrical system is composed of two 24-volt batteries with a 175-ampere-hour capacity for the hull and four 12-volt batteries providing 390-ampere-hour capacity for the turret.

Endurance and Logistics

Despite its large size, the G6 is equipped with two fuel tanks located on either side of the midsection of the hull, with a combined capacity of 700ℓ (185gal). This grants the vehicle an operational range of 700km (435mi) on the road and 350km (217mi) cross-country, allowing for flexible force movement alongside mechanised formations. The G6 can reach a maximum road speed of 85km/h (53mph), though its recommended cruising speed is 70km/h (44mph). Depending on the terrain, the G6 can maintain a cross-country speed of 30–40km/h (19–25mph).

The G6 also features a 150ℓ (40gal) drinking water tank, accessible via a tap located at the rear of the vehicle.

Proven during combat operations in the South African Border War, the G6 can operate in rugged and variable terrain for up to a month with minimal technical and logistical support. The G6-52 variant incorporates improvements to the chassis, simplifying maintenance and extending service intervals, which further enhances the vehicle's endurance.

Vehicle layout

The G6 is operated by a crew of six, namely the commander, layer, breech operator, loader, ammunition handler, and driver. During engagements, the ammunition handler and driver work outside the vehicle at the rear, preparing and passing ammunition to the loader, who operates within the turret.

The driver's compartment is positioned at the front-centre of the vehicle between the two front wheel wells. The driver is equipped with day/night viewing capabilities and enjoys an excellent

G6-45 driveline illustration. (Open source)

180-degree field-of-view through three large bulletproof windows. During combat, an armoured shield can be activated, which pops up to cover the front window for added protection. In this mode, the driver relies on a day periscope for forward visibility. Located behind the driver are the gearbox and engine, with all key engine functions monitored through a comprehensive engine control system at the driver's station. The driver's entry and exit are through a roof hatch above their seat.

The turret is mounted over the two rear axles at the rear of the vehicle, manned by the commander, layer, breech operator, and loader. It is equipped with multiple viewing ports, a Gyro laying sight for indirect fire, and a telescope for direct firing. On the right side of the ordnance, the commander and breech operator are seated, while the layer and loader occupy the left side.

G6-45. AAD 2012. (S. Tegner)

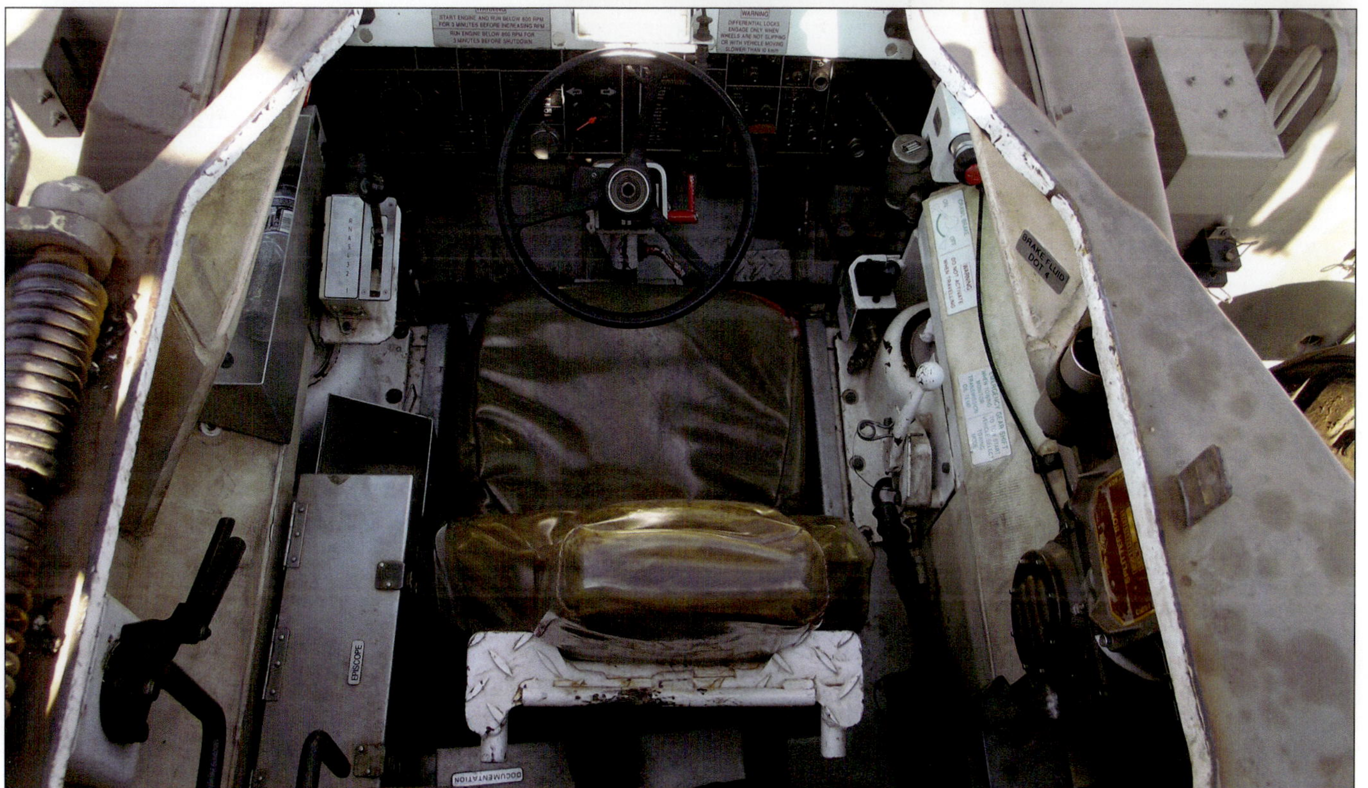

G6-45. Driver's station. AAD 2012. (S. Tegner)

G6-45. Right front driver's station. Triangle nose houses additional shells. AAD 2012. (S. Tegner)

G6-45. Top down view from turret. Note the storage bin on the gun and the bush bracket on the top protecting the measuring equipment used to determine the shell muzzle velocity. AAD 2012. (S. Tegner)

G6-45. Engine deck view. AAD 2012. (S. Tegner)

G6-45. View of the turret top. Note the storage rack in the centre and gunners cupola on the right. AAD 2012. (S. Tegner)

G6-45. Front left side of turret. Note the protective bush bracket over the smoke grenade launchers. AAD 2012. (S. Tegner)

G6-45. Gunner's cupola. An SS-77 general purpose machine gun can be mounted on the bracket. AAD 2012. (S. Tegner)

G6-45. Upper rear of turret. Note the cones for GPS/SATNAV. AAD 2012. (S. Tegner)

G6-45. Interior left side of turret. Seats for the ammunition and breech operator. AAD 2012. (S. Tegner)

G6-45. Interior gunners station in turret. Vertical aim drive (centre), gunner's turret control (right) and gun-laying control (middle right). AAD 2012. (S. Tegner)

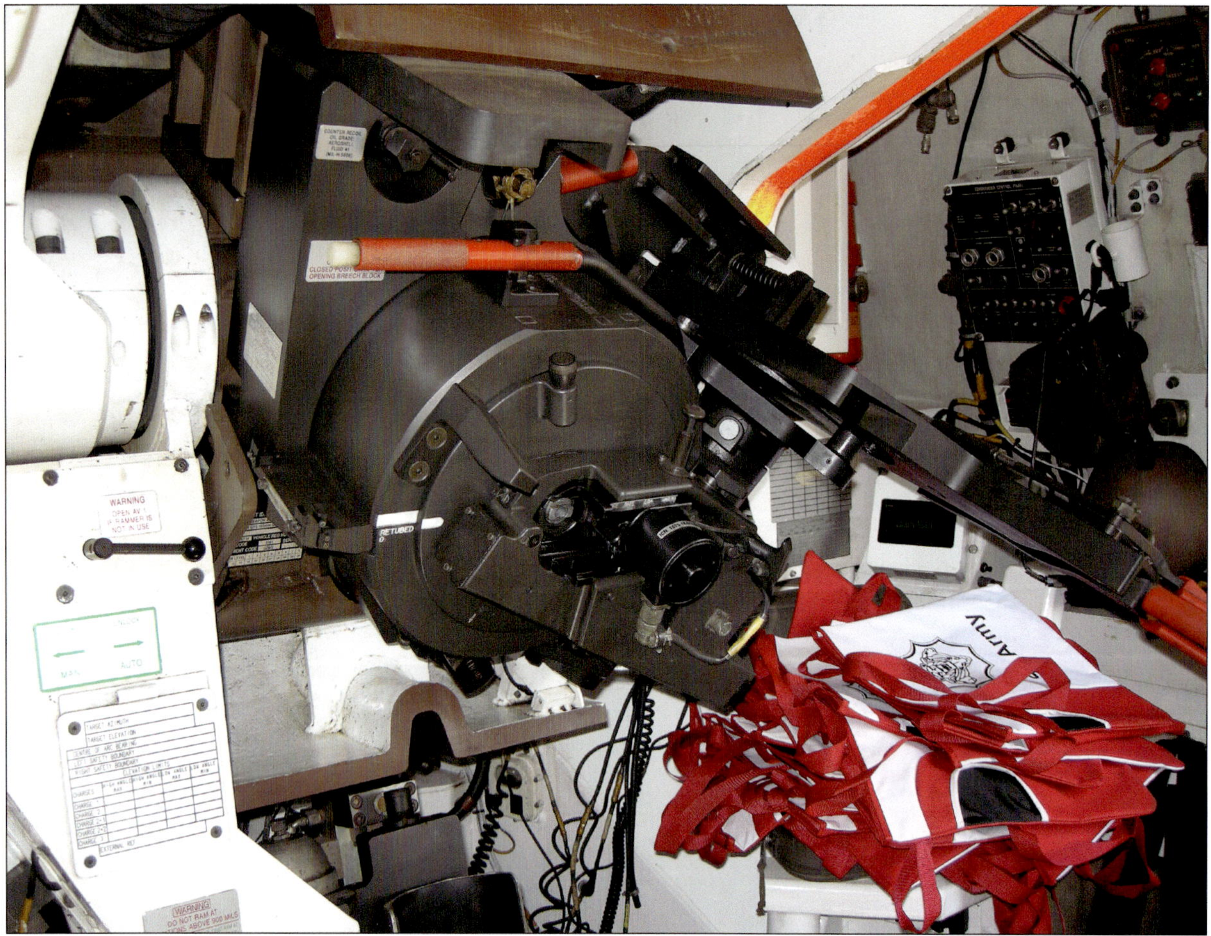

G6-45. Interior turret, gun breach. Firing mechanism manual control lever. AAD 2012. (S. Tegner)

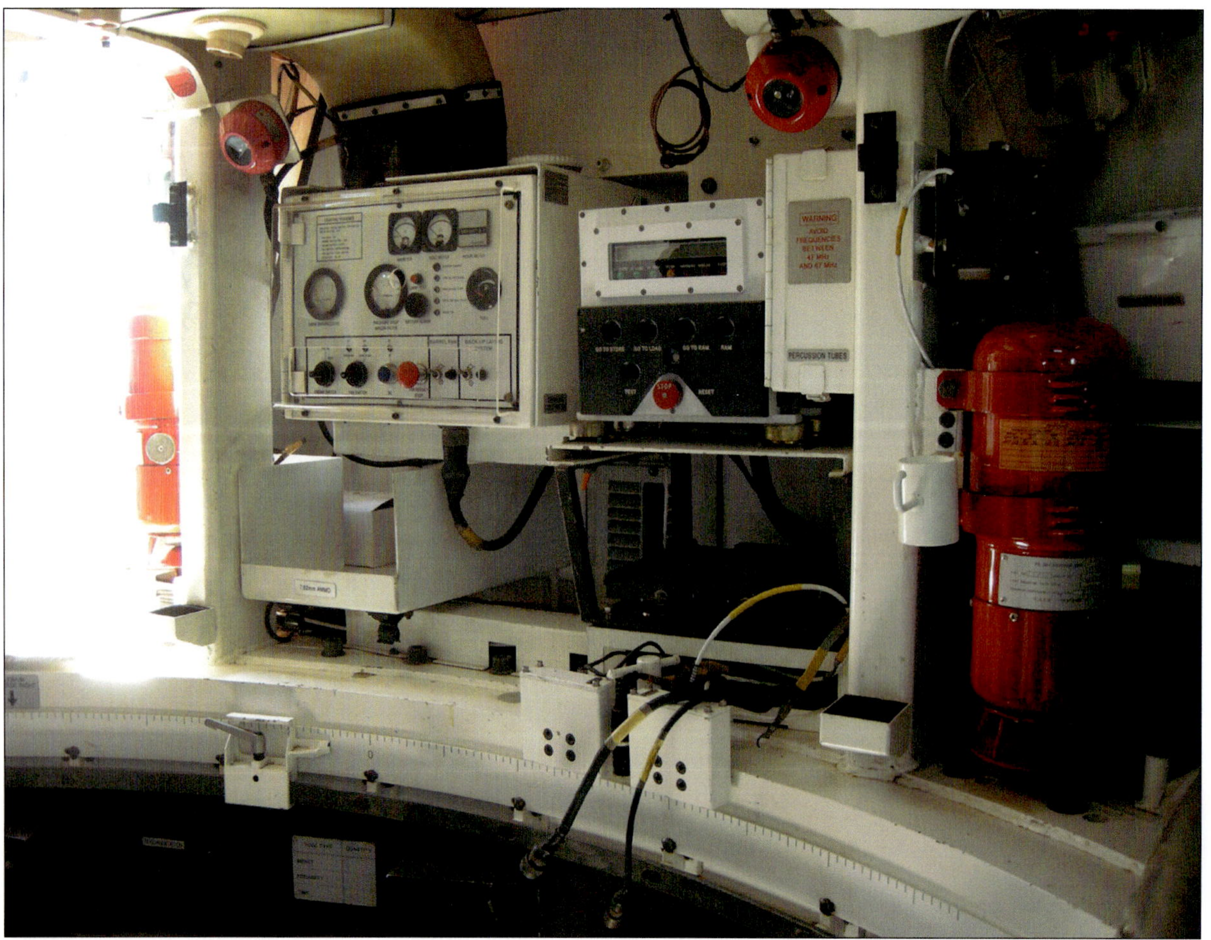

G6-45. Interior turret, radio station rear of turret. AAD 2012. (S. Tegner)

G6-45. Interior turret, projectile and fuse storage. Nineteen storage chambers for projectiles (centre) which are for emergency use in direct combat as first stage ammunition. Fuses are stored in lock boxes (left and right). AAD 2012. (S. Tegner)

G6-45 AAD 2012. Rear hull features exterior blowout panels which are closed. There are nine vertical row blowout panels with four storage tubes each for charges. Loading chute (bottom middle) to the interior with two bays. Exterior projectile storage (bottom row left and right). Rear turret contains the toolkit box (left). APU (left vents) and ACU (right vent). AAD 2014. (S. Tegner)

The commander's station offers basic vehicle control, including the ability to switch off the engine and engage an emergency brake to halt the vehicle. The commander also has access to a cupola, providing a 360-degree field-of-view and a roof hatch for observation or exit.

For air defence, a 12.7mm or 7.62mm BMG can be mounted on the left cupola. Its primary role is to engage low-flying aircraft, lightly armoured vehicles, and to suppress enemy infantry. The G6 can carry up to 2,000 rounds of 7.62mm or 1,000 rounds of 12.7mm ammunition for these defensive weapons.

The turret rear features a dedicated crew access hatch on the right, as well as an ammunition loading hatch at the rear centre, positioned near the floor, allowing for easy resupply of shells from outside. For additional protection, the turret is fitted with two banks of 81mm electrically operated smoke grenade launchers on either side of the front. These can be deployed for concealment or defence. There are also five firing ports (two on the left, two on the right, and one at the rear), enabling the crew to use their R4 rifles for close-quarters defence if necessary.

Main armament

The G6 Rhino's primary armament is a 155mm 45-calibre gun, while its advanced variant, the G6-52, features a longer 155mm 52-calibre gun. One of the factors contributing to the G6's early success in long-range engagements was its blast chamber volume of 23ℓ (6gal), which exceeded the standard international volume of 21ℓ. The G6-52 maintains the same 23ℓ chamber, but the G6-52 ER variant uses an even larger 25ℓ chamber for enhanced range and firepower.

The G6's 155mm gun is fitted with a single-baffle muzzle brake and an upgraded hydro-pneumatic recoil system. It utilises a rammer, enabling a sustained rate of fire of three rounds per minute. The G6-52 variant further enhances this with a barrel cooling fan system, a multi-baffle muzzle brake, and a new rammer, which doubles the rate of fire to six rounds per minute. The breech mechanism of the G6 consists of an interrupted screw stepped-thread, while the G6-52 employs a more advanced combination swingblock with mushroom head and sliding block system. The gun's elevation ranges from -5 to +75 degrees, with a 40-degree traverse to either side.

The G6 carries between 39 and 41 projectiles, 50 charges, 60 primers, and 39 fuses, with 18 backup fuses. Of these, 19 projectiles are stored inside the turret's fighting compartment for emergency use. Eight projectiles are positioned on either side of the vehicle's nose, while an additional four projectiles, along with most of the charges, are kept in exterior compartments at the rear of the hull. These compartments, known as blast-out magazines, are used first when the vehicle is in a stationary firing position. The G6-52 variant employs a carousel that holds 40 projectiles and 40 charges for quicker and more efficient loading.

All ammunition used by the G6 is developed in South Africa and supplied by Rheinmetall Denel Munitions. The G6 is compatible with all standard NATO 155mm ammunition, in addition to the specialised M1 series Extended Range Full Bore (ERFB) and Extended Range Full Bore-Base Bleed (ERFB-BB) ammunition, which extends its range.

The G6 uses the M64 modular charge system (MCS), which enables the gun to achieve a velocity of 909m/s (2,982ft/s) with HE-BB rounds or 911m/s (2,989ft/s) with standard HE rounds. One notable ammunition development is the M9703 Velocity-Enhanced Long-range Artillery Projectile (V-LAP), which combines base-bleed and rocket motor technology developed under Project Assegai. In testing, the G6-52 ER achieved a range of 70km (43.5mi) by firing the M64 MCS and V-LAP combination. However, as of November 2019, the G6-52 set a new benchmark by firing an RDM M9703 V-LAP with an M64 Zone 6 charge, reaching a record distance of 76.3km (47.4mi).

Table 3: G6 variants and ammunition firing ranges

Ammunition	G6-45	G6-52	G6-52 ER
HE without base bleed	30km (18.6mi)	-	-
HE with base bleed	40.5km (25.2mi)	42km (26mi)	50km (31mi)
HE with V-LAP	52.5km (32.6mi)	58km (36mi)	76.2km (47.4mi)
Note: All firing ranges except V-Lap/G6-52 are at sea level			

Fire control system

The FCS of the G6 operates through an indirect targeting process. Targeting data is collected by forward observers and transmitted via the Artillery Target Engagement System (ATES) to a fire control post. This data is then relayed to the individual G6's Launcher Management System (LMS) through a secure frequency-hopping VHF radio link.

For direct-fire missions, the G6 layer manually aims the ordinance using a telescopic sight. The G6-52 variant, however, is equipped with an automatic gun-laying system, making it more advanced in this respect. The G6-52 features the AS2000 automatic fire control system, which integrates a fully automated gun-laying and navigation system the FIN 3110 RLG designed by Denel Land Systems. This system includes a new LMS computer, which combines a fire control computer, GPS receiver, and touchscreen display with Denel Land Systems sensors for improved accuracy and operational efficiency.

One of the most advanced capabilities of the G6-52 is its ability to perform MRSI (Multiple Round Simultaneous Impact) fire missions. By firing several rounds at different trajectories, the shells can strike the target simultaneously, maximising surprise and effectiveness. This tactic can be executed at ranges up to 50km (31mi).

Although the G6 is capable of firing from a wheeled stance, it is equipped with four hydraulically operated stabiliser legs for added stability during firing. These legs are located between the first and second wheel pairs, as well as behind the rear wheels. The G6 can be deployed to fire within one minute and can move again within the same time, allowing for 'shoot and scoot' tactics, which are essential for evading counter-battery fire.

Protection

The G6 Rhino features all-welded steel alloy armour, protecting against small arms fire, ballistic fragments, and explosive concussions across its entire chassis. The vehicle's frontal arc, including the turret, is capable of withstanding hits from 20mm AP rounds, ensuring a high degree of survivability against light-to-medium threats.

The turret includes several firing ports that allow the crew to use their personal weapons for close-in defence. Like many South African-produced military vehicles, the G6 has built-in mine protection. Its chassis is designed to resist mine blasts, with a double-layered floor that offers protection against multiple mine explosions. The G6 can withstand up to three TM-57 anti-tank mine anti-tank mine blast equivalent to 21kg (41lbs) of TNT detonations under the hull, a vital feature for operations in mine-laden environments.

In terms of protection against chemical, biological, and radiological threats, the G6 features an overpressure system to protect the crew. The G6-52 further improves upon this by offering full NBC protection, enhancing the crew's survivability in contaminated environments. Additionally, the G6 is equipped with an automatic fire-extinguishing system, which ensures rapid response in the event of an onboard fire.

G6 Family

G6 SPAAM

When the Rooikat ZA-35 SPAAG (self-propelled anti-aircraft gun) and SPAAM (self-propelled anti-aircraft missile) projects (covered in Volume 2) were cancelled, an attempt was made to revive the SPAAM concept using the G6 platform. A mock-up was created, featuring a wooden turret structure as a demonstrator. This effort aimed to explore the possibilities of bridging the gap between existing technologies and potential solutions for air defence. Although no ammunition was produced for the project, the SAHV-3 missile system would have most likely been integrated into the role if the project had progressed beyond the paper study phase.

Operational History

The G6 has proven its combat effectiveness in two major operational deployments. G6 Rhino was first used operationally during the latter stages of the South African Border War. It demonstrated its superior firepower, mobility, and range, providing critical long-range artillery support that often outgunned and outranged the artillery of the opposing forces, including FAPLA. The G6's ability to deploy quickly and perform effective 'shoot and scoot' tactics was vital to its success in the bush war environment.

Since August 2015, United Arab Emirates-operated G6 units have been actively deployed in the Yemen conflict, supporting operations against Houthi rebels. The G6's long-range precision artillery and ability to operate in challenging desert terrains have made it a key asset in the UAE's military efforts in Yemen, where it continues to demonstrate its durability and combat effectiveness in a modern conflict zone.

The G6 family of vehicles continues to be a versatile and formidable artillery system with proven performance in various combat environments.

Conclusion

Few would disagree that the G6 was ahead of its time when it was first fielded in 1987. The SANDF actively operates nine G6 vehicles, while the remaining 34 are in preservation storage during peacetime. Characterised by its impressive fire range, mobility, speed, accuracy, and endurance, the G6 remains at the forefront when compared to other wheeled and tracked self-propelled howitzers worldwide. Its original design objectives of long-range fire, mobility, flexibility, and efficient logistics have been further enhanced by the G6's emphasis on crew protection. Through continued upgrades, the G6 remains a formidable force in the realm of self-propelled howitzer vehicles, with a bright future ahead in modern artillery warfare. Its adaptability and ongoing modernisation ensure that the G6 continues to be a reliable and effective asset for the SANDF and other armed forces that utilise it.

6

Ystervark

The Ystervark takes its Afrikaans name from the South African or 'Cape' porcupine, a strong, resilient animal protected by an array of spines used to defend itself. Like its namesake, the Ystervark SPAAG was a robust vehicle, evolved to operate effectively in the harsh Southern African environment.

Development

By 1983/84, the SADF's Anti-Aircraft Regiments were using towed artillery, primarily the GAI-CO1 20mm anti-aircraft guns. With the transition to mobile warfare, the need for a self-propelled anti-aircraft vehicle became evident. The first attempts to create such a vehicle involved mounting a GAI-CO1 gun on a Mercedes-Benz gun tractor, secured with wooden railway sleepers. While crude, these early testbeds helped establish operational requirements for a mine-resistant, mobile anti-aircraft system.

In 1981, Project Sireb had already been initiated to develop mine-resistant vehicles to replace the Buffel APC. One prototype from this project, known as the Bulldog, was adopted by the SAAF for airfield patrols and later became the foundation for the Ystervark. This led to the development of a new mobile, mine-resistant vehicle that could accompany mechanised battalions on combat operations.

The Ystervark was first deployed during Exercise Thunder Chariot in 1984 and saw its first combat use with 32 Bn in 1986. The vehicle played a vital role in operations Moduler, Hooper, and Excite in Angola, deterring low-altitude air attacks by Angolan and Cuban aircraft. Notably, Ystervarks shot down two MiG-23 jets, one on 8 October 1987 and another on 17 March 1988, during the Battle of Cuito Cuanavale.

Though successful, the Ystervark was phased out in 1991, replaced by the SAMIL 100 Kwêvoël Bosvark SPAAG. It was officially decommissioned in 1997. It is estimated that around 70 Ystervarks were produced, and they remained exclusive to the SADF.

Mercedes-Benz gun tractor. Fitted with the GAI-CO1 20mm AA gun on the back while shooting at Toothrock. 10 Anti-Aircraft Regiment (Youngsfield Facebook group)

Ystervark. Exercise Thunder Chariot 1984. (Photo collection J. Van Zyl)

Design Features

The Ystervark was specifically designed for mine protection and survivability in hostile environments. Key features included high ground clearance, a V-shaped underbelly to deflect mine blasts, and a reinforced structure to minimise the risk of hull damage. While the chassis-based MPV design did not offer the same level of protection as modern monocoque hull designs, it allowed for easier field repairs and reduced the logistical burden.

Mobility

Built on the SAMIL 20 chassis, the Ystervark was designed for rugged off-road conditions. Its ground clearance of 460mm (18.1in) allowed it to tackle difficult terrain, and it could ford up to 1.2m (3.9ft) of water. Powered by a 124hp (93kW) Deutz 6-cylinder air-cooled engine, the vehicle had a power-to-weight ratio of 20.4hp/t.

The Ystervark featured single-leaf springs on the front axle and double-coil springs on the rear axle, ensuring stable off-road performance. Its 14.50×20 tires provided the necessary traction, and the vehicle's permanent 4×4 drive enhanced its cross-country mobility. The suspension system and portal axle configuration allowed it to cross a 0.85m (33in) ditch with ease.

Endurance and logistics

The Ystervark had a 200ℓ (53gal) fuel tank which granted it an operational range of 950km (590mi) on-road and 475km (295mi) off-road. Its maximum road speed was 90km/h (55mph) and 30km/h (19mph) off-road. A modular design allowed for easier maintenance and reduced logistical requirements. Additionally, the domestic production of components made replacement easy and lowered the cost for parts. A 100ℓ (26gal) freshwater tank was located inside the V-shaped hull for the crew and was accessible via a tap located at the rear left of the lower vehicle's V-shape.

Vehicle layout

The Ystervark was based on the SAMIL 20 chassis, known for its off-road capabilities. The chassis was fitted with a portal driving axle and pneumatically lockable differential. This arrangement allowed it to tackle difficult terrain with permanent 4×4 wheel drive. The engine was located at the front of the vehicle, directly behind the bumper and below the driver's compartment, which centralised the weight distribution and allowed easy access for maintenance or replacement. Between the engine and the driver's compartment was the transmission system, a five-speed (four forward, one reverse) synchromesh manual gearbox. This configuration was coupled to the transfer case, ensuring optimal gear shifting in various terrain conditions.

The driver's cab was mounted on the front right-hand side of the vehicle, offering basic protection with 7mm thick armoured plating. The design prioritised protection from small arms fire and shrapnel while keeping the overall vehicle weight manageable. Three rectangular bulletproof windows, one front-facing and two side-facing, provided the driver with visibility. These windows were angled slightly outward to minimise reflective glare, enhancing visibility without compromising protection. The cab was covered by an unarmoured high-density polyethylene roof. The entrance to the driver's compartment was a single door located on the right side of the cab, accessible via two steel steps. Inside, the driver's seat was blast resistant and equipped with a harness to protect against spinal injuries in the event of a mine detonation.

The gear selector stick was located on the driver's left-hand side, allowing easy shifting while maintaining control of the vehicle. Communication between the driver and the rest of the crew, especially the commander, was facilitated through a small opening in the rear of the cab.

The weapons deck, situated behind the driver's cab and atop the chassis, was the centrepiece of the Ystervark's design. The main armament, a GAI-CO1 20mm anti-aircraft gun, was mounted centrally on a three-legged support structure on the deck. This allowed for a 360-degree traverse and flexible engagement of targets in all directions. The weapon itself was gas-operated, and the gunner manually controlled its operation from his seat.

The crew seating was located between the driver's cab and the weapons deck. Two seats were arranged side-by-side, facing backward toward the gun. The commander sat on the left seat, directly behind the driver's cab, which allowed him to relay commands to the driver. The gunner sat on the right seat, from where he operated the gun. Both crew members were secured by harnesses to protect against vehicle rollover or mine detonations. These seats were mounted slightly higher than the driver's seat, giving the crew a better view of the surroundings during combat.

Access to the weapons deck was provided by steel steps located above the rear wheels on either side of the vehicle. The left and right sides of the weapons deck featured hinged armour panels, which could be lowered to allow the gun to engage targets. When not in use, these panels were secured in their upright positions to protect the crew and equipment. The left and right panels could fold down completely, while the middle-left panel was limited to a 45-degree drop.

At the rear of the weapons deck was a large storage box constructed from high-density polyethylene. This box was divided into compartments, with the lower section used by the passengers for storing kits and equipment, while the upper section was reserved for the driver's use.

A spare wheel was mounted to the left of the driver's cab, providing quick access in the event of a flat tyre or damage in the field. For communication, an A-53 UHF radio set was installed on the weapons deck between the commander and gunner seats, allowing for tactical coordination with other units.

Armament

The Ystervark's primary weapon was the GAI-CO1 20mm anti-aircraft gun, mounted on the rear weapons deck. This gas-operated gun fired at a rate of 550 rounds per minute from a 75-round magazine. The weapon had an effective range of 2,000m (2,187yd), and its ammunition types include HE and APHE which can engage low-flying aircraft, helicopters, and lightly armoured vehicles. The APHE rounds were capable of penetrating 15mm (0.59in) of RHA at 800m (875yd).

Fire control system

The mount traditionally included an x1 sight for antiaircraft use and an x3.7 sight for ground targets. The Ystervark was fitted with a Delta IV reflector sight, adjustable for target speeds ranging from 200km/h (124mph) to 900km/h (559mph). This sight could be illuminated at night, allowing for effective target engagement in low-light conditions.

Protection

The Ystervark's V-shaped bottom armour design deflected the energy of mine blasts away from the hull, protecting the crew from a single TM-57 anti-tank mine blast equivalent to 6.34kg (14lbs) of TNT under the hull, or a double stack under any wheel equivalent to 12.6kg (27.7lbs) TNT. Its bulletproof windows and 7mm (0.27in) thick side armour provided protection against 7.62×51mm NATO and 7.62×39mm AK-47 ball ammunition, as well as shrapnel from explosive devices. However, the rear and top of the weapons deck were left exposed.

Ystervark. (Open source)

Operational Use and Doctrine

In 1986, Ystervarks were deployed in troop-sized units of six vehicles, assigned to mechanised battalions such as 32, 61, and 62 Battalions. Their primary role was to provide anti-aircraft protection, though the limitations of manual aiming and small magazine capacity meant they were most effective when operating in groups. Despite these limitations, the Ystervark's presence forced enemy aircraft to fly at higher altitudes, significantly reducing the effectiveness of air attacks on SADF ground forces.

The operational doctrine established in 1987 emphasised the Ystervark's position within the mechanised columns, typically moving one tactical jump (100–200m) behind the A Echelon or flanking the advancing force. This positioning was strategic, anticipating enemy air attacks from the flanks, a common threat in mechanised combat. Although the Ystervark's main armament faced backwards and required it to be stationary to engage targets, this limitation did not prevent its effective deployment. The vehicle's role was primarily focused on protecting advancing columns and critical assets such as headquarters, medical units, artillery, and supplies. Its key strength was its ability to redeploy swiftly, within 10 minutes, making it an adaptable and responsive asset in fast-moving operations.

In 1989, the doctrine was formally introduced to the AA School and 101 Battery, 10 AA Regiment,

Ystervark. Exercise Thunder Chariot 1984. (Photo collection J. Van Zyl)

culminating in an updated AA Battle Handling doctrine that shaped future operations. While the Ystervark's primary function was defensive, it did see one conventional combat role during the 'advance to contact' in September 1987. In this instance, during an engagement with FAPLA's 47 Brigade, the Ystervark was deployed alongside 61 Mechanised Battalion to protect the flanks of the force. With no enemy aircraft present, the vehicle successfully engaged visible vehicles, soft targets, and infantry, showcasing its flexibility and effectiveness in ground combat as part of a mechanised unit.

Conclusion

When the SADF transitioned from motorised to mechanised warfare, it needed a SPAAG capable of keeping pace with its mechanised units. The Ystervark was developed as a stopgap solution to meet this requirement. In terms of mobility, the Ystervark successfully matched the speed and manoeuvrability of the mechanised units it supported.

However, its main armament had two key limitations: a limited number of rounds per magazine and the necessity for manual aiming, which hindered its effectiveness against fast-moving jet aircraft. These shortcomings were somewhat mitigated by deploying the Ystervark in troops of six vehicles, allowing for concentrated firepower and increased operational flexibility.

Despite its limitations, the Ystervark posed a credible threat to enemy aircraft, forcing them to operate at higher altitudes during bombing runs. This resulted in significantly reduced accuracy and bombing success. Without the Ystervark, Cuban and Soviet air-to-ground attacks on SADF mechanised forces in Angola would likely have been far more aggressive and effective.

The Ystervark also served as the official combat vehicle for anti-aircraft formation training and exercises at 101 Battery, 10 AA Regiment.

Ystervark crew from 32 Battalion with the external 800ℓ fuel drop tank of a MiG-23ML which they shot down in 1987. (L. Scheepers)

7

Bateleur Multiple Rocket Launcher

The Bateleur FV2 was developed in 1983 to replace its smaller predecessor, the Visarend (Fish Eagle) FV1. Its primary role was to provide the SADF with first-strike capabilities in support of the artillery strategy outlined in 1974. Built to operate in the African battlespace, the Bateleur was designed to handle the unique challenges of the terrain and combat environment experienced during the South African Border War, making it a powerful and reliable addition to the artillery forces.

Development

The development of a South African MRL system began in 1974 under Project Furrow at the CSIR, which led to the creation of the Visarend which was also known as the Valkiri. The SADF recognised the threat posed by the Soviet BM-21 Grad MRL, which could fire 122mm rockets to a range of 20km (12.3mi), far beyond the reach of most South African artillery systems at the time. The BM-21 could saturate a large area with high-explosive rockets in seconds, whereas an entire artillery battery (eight guns) would be required

to achieve the same effect in the same timeframe. The Visarend, with its 127mm (5in) rockets, could outrange the BM-21 by 12km (7.5mi), thanks to its superior rocket motor. A 127mm size was selected as it was the same diameter used for the V3 air-to-air missile by Kentron (later Denel Somchem), simplifying development with only a few modifications. The Visarend played a key role in several operations such as Operation Protea, Alpha Centauri, and Moduler, but it lacked the durability needed for the rough terrain and was vulnerable to landmine threats.

To address these shortcomings, work began on the Bateleur in the mid-1980s under Project Canton, with production completed in 1986. Somchem led the development, with technical assistance from Denel and ARMSCOR. The first Bateleur vehicles were fielded just as the South African Border War was coming to a close in 1989. The Bateleur is still in service with the SANDF, though four of the 25 vehicles produced are currently in preservation storage. At the time of writing, the Bateleur is undergoing an upgrade to its rocket laying and navigation systems under Project Topstar.

Bateleur FV2. Ripple fire at Army Battle School Lohatla. (Open source)

Visarend FV1. Exercise Thunder Chariot 1984. (Photo collection J. Van Zyl)

Design Features

The Bateleur was designed to address the limitations of the Visarend, including insufficient protection and poor mobility over rough terrain. The Bateleur is a 3-axle, 6x6 all-wheel-drive MRL, equipped with 40 tubes and based on the robust SAMIL Kwêvoël 100 with a mine-protected body. The hull underneath the crew cabin features a V-shaped design to deflect mine blasts away from the cabin, enhancing survivability.

The primary mission of the Bateleur is to destroy high-value targets (HVTs) and high impact targets (HITs), including counter-battery strikes against enemy artillery and air defence emplacements.

Mobility

The Bateleur features a six-wheel configuration, offering greater reliability and easier maintenance compared to tracked vehicles. It is powered by a Deutz FIOL 413 V10 air-cooled diesel engine, producing 268hp (200kW) at 2,650rpm, providing a 12.5hp/t power-to-weight ratio. This power allows the Bateleur to achieve a maximum road speed of 90km/h (56mph) and 30km/h (18.6mph) off-road.

The Bateleur can ford 1.2m (3.9ft) of water without preparation and cross a 0.5m (19.7in) ditch at a crawl. The vehicle features a WITHINGS suspension system and offers a 355mm (13.9in) ground clearance. It also has power steering, with acceleration and braking operated via foot pedals, making the driver's task easier.

Endurance and logistics

The Bateleur is designed for strategic mobility, with two 200ℓ (53gal) diesel fuel tanks, providing an operational range of 600km (373mi) on roads, 350km (217mi) cross-country, and 175km (108mi) over-sand. Additionally, the vehicle is equipped with a 200ℓ (53gal) water tank located beneath the crew compartment, which can be accessed via a tap located above the front left wheel.

The rear launcher of the Bateleur carries 40x127mm (5in) rockets in launch tubes. Rockets are supplied by a SAMIL Kwêvoël 100 ammunition truck, which carries 96 rockets and provides personnel to assist with the reloading process.

Vehicle layout

The Bateleur can be divided into two main components: the vehicle which includes the body, crew cabin, and drivetrain and the weapon system which comprises the mounting, cradle, tube pack, sighting, laying system, and stabilisers.

The engine is located at the front of the vehicle, with the raised crew cabin positioned behind it. The vehicle's body is built on a V-shaped hull, which provides protection against mine blasts from underneath. The engine is equipped with a trapezoidal ventilation grid at the front of the hood, and a V-shaped bumper is positioned beneath it to assist with bundu bashing (driving through dense bush). The crew cabin is rectangular, with two forward-facing rectangular windows and two armoured entry and exit doors on either side, each equipped with a bulletproof window. The roof is armoured to protect against medium artillery fragments, offering all-round protection against small arms fire.

Access to the crew cabin is provided by a chain ladder on either side. At the rear of the vehicle, hydraulically operated stabiliser legs are deployed when the launcher is to be fired.

The Bateleur's crew consists of six members: the Driver Station (Bombardier/Lance Bombardier) is located on the forward right side of the cabin, responsible for driving the vehicle and navigating rough terrain. The Crew Commander (Sergeant) is seated on the forward left and oversees the operation. Behind them, the layer

(Lance Bombardier) is responsible for laying and orientating the launcher, while the 2IC (Bombardier) sits in the centre, assisting with operations. The Ammunition Loader and Gunner (Lance Bombardier) is positioned on the left side of the cabin, aiding in reloading and operating the weaponry. The vehicle commander manages communications through the AS2000 Command system, and the driver assists in rocket reloading when not operating the vehicle. The layer is tasked with aligning the launcher, while the Bombardier mans the roof-mounted 7.62mm BMG for close protection while in the crew cabin.

Main armament

The Bateleur's launcher carries 40x127mm (5in) rockets, stored in two packs of 5x4 launcher tubes. The rockets are fired in 0.5-second intervals, with a full salvo lasting 20 seconds. The launcher is electro-hydraulically operated via a joystick, capable of elevating up to 50

Bateleur FV2. Front view AAD 2024. (D. Venter)

Bateleur FV2. Rear view AAD 2024. (D. Venter)

Bateleur FV2 driver's cabin. Commander sits left adjacent to the fire control station which is secured in the bracket. AAD 2022. (D. Venter)

degrees and traversing 90 degrees to the left and 19 degrees to the right, depending on the elevation.

At sea level, the standard 127mm rocket has a minimum range of 7.5km (4.7mi) with a large drag ring, and a maximum range of 22.5km (13.9mi) without a drag ring. Experimental long-range rockets, with a range of 37km (22.9mi), have been tested. A standard HE-Frag rocket is 2.95m (9.67ft) long, weighs 62kg (137lbs), and contains 8,500 x 5.5mm (0.21in) steel balls cast in a resin sleeve filled with an RDX/TNT mix. These rockets can detonate on direct contact or via a proximity fuse, depending on the tactical needs and nature of the target. A salvo of six Bateleurs firing 10 rockets each can hit a 350m x 250m (383yd x 273yd) target area, delivering 516,000 high-velocity steel balls in five seconds, which would be lethal to all unarmoured targets.

The launcher is integrated with the South African-developed SAA ATES, which handles tactical, terminal, and technical fire control, as well as individual launcher control through appropriate hardware and software with integrated digital communication. The selection of rockets, sequence, and arming is controlled from a panel on the dashboard.

At the rear of the vehicle, a platform can slide out, providing an elevated position for handling and loading rockets. Loading the launcher involves sliding a rocket into each of the 40 tubes, a process that takes 15 to 20 minutes. However, a well-trained crew can be ready to fire again in just three minutes. For close protection, the vehicle can be equipped with a 7.62mm SS-77 GPMG mounted on the roof of the crew cabin.

Table 4: Bateleur firing range

127mm (5in) rocket	No drag ring	Small drag ring	Medium drag ring	Large drag ring
Standard	12–22.5km (7.5–13.9mi)	9–15km (5.6–9.3mi)	8–11.5km (4.9–7.1mi)	7–9.5km (4.3–5.9mi)
Extended range	19.6–37km (12.2–22.9mi)	*14.7–24.6km (9.1–15.3mi)	*13–18.9km (8.1–11.7mi)	*11.4–15.6km (7.1–9.7mi)

Note: All firing ranges are at sea level

*Estimated ranges based on the drag ratio for a standard rocket

Fire control system

Once a target has been acquired by the appropriate target acquisition resource and analysed, the decision to engage is made at the relevant artillery tactical headquarters. Orders are then issued for the launcher(s) to move to a designated loading area where they are loaded while the firing position is reconnoitred and prepared. Once ready, the launcher(s) are moved to the firing position, where they are accurately oriented on a selected bearing, typically at the centre of the target area. The ATES computer in the Fire Control Post determines the bearing and range to the target and computes the necessary ballistic corrections to compensate for the existing non-standard conditions. The firing data is then transmitted to the launcher(s) in the form of a fire order (FO), detailing the bearing and elevation at which the launcher pack should be laid, drag ring confirmation, the number of rounds to be fired, and the time on target. After firing, the launcher(s) immediately vacate the firing position (a shoot and scoot tactic) to avoid being spotted by the enemy due to the distinctive launch signature of any MRL system.

Protection

The crew cabin of the Bateleur is protected all around from 7.62mm small arms fire, and the roof is rated for medium fragmentation protection. The V-shaped hull has been tested and proven to withstand the impact of three TM-57 landmines or the equivalent of 21kg (46lbs) of TNT beneath the crew cabin, providing robust protection for the vehicle and its crew in mine-laden environments.

Conclusion

The Bateleur fulfils a niche role in the SANDF as a medium MRL. It was designed based on the same core principles that characterise other South African wheeled military vehicles, focusing on long-range firepower, speed, mobility, flexibility, and ease of logistics. While the Bateleur has not yet been deployed in active combat, the firepower it brings to the battlefield is formidable. The ability to deliver a concentrated and devastating salvo of rockets in a short amount of time provides a significant tactical advantage, making it a powerful asset in the SANDF's artillery arsenal.

127mm (5in) rocket. AAD 2018. (D. Venter)

127mm rocket. Cut out showing the high-velocity steel balls. AAD 2024. (D. Venter)

8

Olifant Mk1A Main Battle Tank

The Olifant Mk1A MBT was a critical evolution in South Africa's armoured capabilities, designed to address the unique challenges of warfare in the African battlespace. Developed during a time of increasing geopolitical isolation and technological embargoes, the Olifant Mk1A represents a remarkable blend of innovation and adaptation. Emerging from the need to modernise South Africa's ageing fleet of Centurion tanks, the Olifant Mk1A was built to deliver the mobility, firepower, and protection required to face modern threats. Its creation not only reflects South Africa's ingenuity in military vehicle design but also underscores its ability to convert older platforms into effective, battle-ready systems.

Development

The Olifant Mk1A represents the final evolutionary stage of South Africa's Centurion tanks before the Cold War's conclusion. In 1953, as part of the Commonwealth, South Africa purchased 87 Mk3 and 116 Mk5 Centurions from Great Britain shortly after the Korean ceasefire. The first Centurion (R74783) was received the same year for training at the School of Armour. After the resolution of the Suez crisis, South Africa had no more need for so many Centurions and sold a surplus of 100 in the 1960s to Switzerland (who sold them to Israel) to fund the acquisition of Mirage fighter aircraft from France. The remaining Centurions were primarily used for training and large-scale exercises throughout the decade.

In 1964, an UN-imposed arms embargo complicated the upkeep of South Africa's Centurion fleet, particularly due to difficulties sourcing parts for the Centurion's 650hp (485kW) V-12 Rolls-Royce Meteor engine, which was prone to overheating in Africa's hot climate. The rocky African terrain also caused wear and tear on the tank's road wheels and suspension. This increased South Africa's reliance on self-sufficiency, leading to the establishment of ARMSCOR in 1968 to handle procurement, research, and development. ARMSCOR managed to source diesel engines from General Motors under the guise of agricultural use, but these engines overheated frequently in the African heat. By 1970, General Motors halted supplies after discovering the engines' true purpose. Simultaneously, many of South Africa's neighbours gained independence and some erupted in civil war, which threatened the security of South Africa's borders.

South Africa purchased 41 unserviceable Centurions from Jordan and by 1973, ARMSCOR acquired eight 810hp (604kW) V-12 petrol engines. The latter were fitted to eight hulls mated to a three-speed automatic transmission by Sandock-Austral. Steering tiller bars were replaced by a handlebar system, and this upgrade led to the development of the Skokiaan tanks. Though the engines were powerful, they guzzled fuel, limiting off-road range to just 40km. These modified Centurions served as an interim solution, while ARMSCOR made modifications to 35 Centurion Mk5A in 1974, which became known as Semel. These tanks featured increased fuel capacity, redesigned steering, brakes, and air filters. Despite these improvements, the project was cancelled due to ongoing engine supply issues.

Olifant Mk1A. Exercise Thunder Chariot 1984. (Photo collection J. Van Zyl)

Skokiaan. School of Armour. (D. Venter)

Meanwhile more Centurion tanks were purchased from India and Jordan, although in various states of disrepair. The SAAC requested an upgrade of the Centurion fleet, similar to the Israeli Sho't. This led to the birth of the Olifant MBT project in 1976, with ARMSCOR, South African Technical Service Corps (SATSC), and Barlow's Heavy Engineering collaborating on the design and upgrades. The first Olifant prototype was completed in 1976 followed by two more in 1977. Key changes to the Olifant included a new engine, replacing the original 84mm gun with a 105mm main gun, upgraded sights, communications, ammunition storage, explosion suppression systems, and smoke generators. The Olifant Mk1 was officially introduced in 1978, featuring a 750hp (599kW) diesel engine and semi-automatic transmission. Production ran from 1978 to 1984.

The capture of T-55 tanks, bound for Tanzania, during a port stop in Durban allowed South Africa to trial the Olifant Mk1 against a fairly modern threat. These trials revealed the need for further improvements, which led to the development of the Olifant Mk1A in 1981. Production began in 1983, with the Olifant Mk1A entering service in 1985. This version featured a stabilised 105mm GT-3 gun, a laser rangefinder, and passive night vision, among other enhancements.

Design Features

The Olifant is a prime example of what ingenuity and technical expertise can accomplish. It took a long time and much effort, but by the time we had finished, almost nothing (30%) of the old Centurions remained except the characteristic hulls, turret shells and track skirts.

Major General (retd) Roland de Vries

Mobility

The Olifant Mk1A has 508mm (20in) of ground clearance and can ford 1.2m (3.9ft) of water without preparation. Retaining the Horstman suspension from the Centurion, it features a new rail system allowing the power pack to be replaced quickly in the field, typically within 30 minutes using a crane. The South African environment's fine dust conditions required improved air filters, optimising the use of the Continental 29ℓ turbocharged air-cooled V12 diesel engine, which produces 750hp (559kW). This engine is coupled to a semi-automatic Allison transmission with two forward (low and high range) and one reverse gear, enabling the Olifant Mk1A to reach 45km/h (28mph) on roads, a marked improvement over the Centurion Mk5's 35km/h (22mph). It can accelerate from 0–30km/h (0–19 mph) in 15 seconds on flat terrain, and steering is done via a handlebar system. These upgrades added only 5t to the vehicle, a minor increase given the enhancements made to overall mobility and performance.

Endurance and logistics

The fuel capacity of the Olifant Mk1A was significantly increased to 1,240ℓ (328gal) from the Centurion Mk5's 458ℓ (121gal). As a result, the Olifant Mk1A can travel 350km (217mi) on roads, 240km (149mi) off-road, and 150km (93mi) on sand, far surpassing the Centurion Mk5's range. To support its use in extended operations over rugged terrain, both mechanical and electronic subsystems were made easily accessible for maintenance. The tracks, consisting of 108 links across 24 road wheels (12 per side), had a service life of 300–500km (186–311mi), necessitating regular upkeep. Combat operations in Angola validated the merit of these upgrades, significantly reducing crew fatigue.

The Olifant Mk1A is armed with two 7.62mm BMGs, one coaxial and the other mounted at the commander's cupola. It carries 5,600 rounds of 7.62mm ammunition (28 belts of 200 rounds each). The tank is equipped with tactical radios for reliable command and control, especially effective in the dense Angolan bush, increasing its battlefield utility. Each tank carried extra whip aerials in a hull tube, as the aerials tended to bend during rough terrain navigation.

Olifant Mk1A. Armed Forces Day 2018. (C. Hugo)

Olifant Mk1A. SA Armour Museum Open Day 2023. (D. Venter)

Additionally, the crew carried jerry cans of water, a cooking stove, tool kits, a tow bar, cables, and spare parts, and relied on daily replenishment from support vehicles.

Vehicle layout

The Olifant Mk1A operates with a four-person crew consisting of a commander, gunner, loader, and driver. The commander's station is located on the right side of the turret and retains the Centurion's 360-degree cupola, which has eight vision blocks and an additional independent vision block. The commander and gunner access their stations through the commander's hatch, while the loader, positioned on the left side of the turret, uses a separate hatch. The gunner's station is located just below the commander's station at the front of the turret. The driver, positioned at the front right of the hull, has a 90-degree forward view through two episcopes and can access his station through a hatch above his seat.

Main armament

The Olifant Mk1A was originally equipped with a 105mm L7 rifled gun barrel sourced from Israel. Later, an improved South African-produced 105mm GT-3B 52-calibre semi-automatic QF gun, manufactured by LEW, was fitted. This upgrade increased the tank's firepower and its adaptability for various types of ammunition.

The GT-3B 105mm gun initially used Israeli-sourced rounds such as the L52A3 APDS, M456 HEAT, and M156 HESH. The L52A3 APDS had a velocity of 1,326m/s (4,350ft/s) and could penetrate 300mm (11.8in) of RHA at a zero-degree angle. The M456 HEAT round had a velocity of 1,000m/s (3,281ft/s) and could effectively penetrate 420mm (16.54in) of RHA, while the M156 HESH round had a velocity of 731m/s (2,398ft/s) and can penetrate 310mm (12.2in) of RHA.

In the mid-1980s, South Africa acquired the Israeli M111 APFSDS-T round, which became the principal anti-tank round for the Olifant Mk1A. The M111 has a muzzle velocity of 1,455m/s (4,773ft/s) and can penetrate 390mm (15.35in) of RHA. It proved highly effective during combat in Angola, where it was used successfully against Soviet T-55 and T-62 tanks, although it could not penetrate the T-72A's frontal turret. The round, known locally as the Fin Mk1, was one of the SADF's most successful anti-tank munitions.

In the mid-1990s, the M429, a second-generation APFSDS-T round, also known as the M2A1 Mk2 or Fin Mk2 Improved, was introduced. This round has a muzzle velocity of 1,450m/s (4,757ft/s) and can penetrate 420mm (16.54in) of RHA at zero degrees.

The M111 was later replaced by the M426, a third-generation APFSDS-T round produced by Rheinmetall Denel Munitions and introduced in 2011. Known as the Fin Mk3, it can penetrate 450mm (17.72in) of RHA at zero degrees with a velocity of 1,450m/s (4,757ft/s) and maintain accuracy at ranges up to 2km (1.24mi).

In addition to anti-tank rounds, the Olifant Mk1A can fire the Denel M9210 HE round, which contained a TNT/HNS filling and had an effective blast radius of 17m (56ft). It has a muzzle velocity of 700m/s (2,296ft/s) and could reach a maximum range of 9km (5.6mi). The M416 white phosphorus round, used for creating smoke screens, can also be fired, reaching a range of 9km (5.6mi) with a muzzle velocity of 730m/s (2,395ft/s).

A new electrical gun and turret drive system were developed for the Olifant Mk1A, along with improved gun stabilisation. The turret drive allowed for 360-degree turret traversal in 20 seconds. The redesigned fighting compartment also improved the layout of the 105mm ammunition storage, increasing its total carrying capacity to 72 rounds, significantly more than the Centurion Mk13's 64-round capacity.

Fire control system

The FCS of the Olifant Mk1A was significantly improved, allowing for quicker and more accurate engagements. The original Centurion's x6 magnification stadia sight was replaced with the Eloptro MSZ-2, a two-channel day and night sight that enhanced the tank's combat effectiveness. The right-hand sight channel provided x8 magnification for daytime use, while the left-hand channel offered x7.2 magnification via an image-intensifier night elbow, greatly improving visibility in low-light conditions.

A co-mounted laser rangefinder, accurate up to 10km, further enhanced target acquisition. The rangefinder's data was fed into a split range drum, which applied the necessary elevation to the main gun based on the target's distance. Testing showed the system to be highly accurate, achieving precision within 50cm x 50cm (19.6in x 19.6in) at 2km (1.24mi). This accuracy was well-suited for the South African *Lowveld* (open grass plains) but proved over-engineered for the typical 100m (109yd) engagements encountered in the dense Angolan bush during combat operations. Despite this, the enhanced FCS represented a significant leap forward in South Africa's armoured warfare capabilities.

Protection

The Olifant Mk1A retained the original Centurion armour configuration, providing a robust yet dated level of protection. It featured 76mm (2.99in) of armour on the frontal glacis, angled at 58 degrees for enhanced deflection, and 152mm (6in) on the frontal turret, providing substantial resistance to direct hits. The side armour was 51mm (2in), the top armour 40mm (1.57in), and the rear was protected by 29mm (1.14in) of armour.

To improve protection, South African-made 4.5mm (0.17in) armoured steel side skirts were added to the vehicle. These skirts were designed to detonate High Explosive Anti-Tank (HEAT) rounds before they could penetrate the hull, enhancing the tank's survivability in combat. Despite these improvements, the Olifant Mk1A remained vulnerable to more advanced threats. Though its 105mm gun could penetrate the frontal armour of T-54/55 and T-62 tanks at a range of 2km (1.24mi), the Olifant Mk1A was still susceptible to their 100mm and 115mm guns, which could destroy it in return. Additionally, the tank remained vulnerable to RPG-7s, a common anti-tank weapon in combat zones.

For additional protection and tactical flexibility, the Olifant Mk1A was equipped with two banks of four 81mm smoke grenade launchers, mounted on either side of the turret. These launchers replaced the older Centurion Mk5 and Mk7 models and allowed the tank to generate smoke screens for concealment during manoeuvres. In later upgrades, the tank also received a protective frame to guard against damage from vegetation while bundu bashing through dense terrain.

The Olifant Family
ARV

At least one Armoured Recovery Vehicle (ARV) based on the hull of the Olifant Mk1 was completed by OMC in 1979, with an additional two ready by 1984 for use in Exercise Thunder Chariot. The primary role of the Olifant ARV was to extract disabled vehicles under enemy fire. The ARV featured a spade ground anchor at the rear, which enabled its main winch, equipped with a 58kW (78hp) motor, to pull a 120-ton load using a 3:1 snatch block. The vehicle also included an excavator digging arm on the rear-right, enhancing its utility in recovery operations.

The ARV had a crew of four, equipped with various tools, including jacks, cables, chains, power saws, spades, and an oxyacetylene cutting and welding torch, all stored in exterior side bins. Additionally, the ARV could be fitted with a small crane jib at the rear to tow damaged vehicles. The vehicle was an essential asset for armoured units, with one ARV assigned per tank squadron and four per tank regiment. The ARVs were initially assigned to 61 Mech. A total of 14 ARVs were built.

Mine-clearing rollers and plough kit

The SADF and SANDF evaluated the use of mine-clearing rollers and plough kits for the Olifant Mk1A. However, the southern African terrain proved challenging for these systems. Tests of plough-type, electro-hydraulic dozer blades revealed they were not feasible, as the test models bent when operating in the hard soil and failed to uproot trees effectively. Additionally, the extra strain on the engine caused overheating, particularly on sandy terrain, making these attachments impractical for extended operations.

Olifant Mk1 ARV. Exercise Thunder Chariot 1984. (Photo collection J. Van Zyl)

Olifant Mk1A. Mine-clearing rollers equipped. (A. Retief)

The Contributions of South African Armour to the Operations of 1987/88 Moduler, Hooper, Packer, Excite and Hilti

Brigadier General (retd) André Retief, who was a major at the time commanding the tank echelon, provides an overview of the use of armour during 1987/88.

Armour's contribution

Armour contributed the following towards the operations:

- AC (Eland 90) Squadron to Sector 10 Oskati
- AC/Anti-Tank (Ratel 90) Squadron to 32 Bn (the only one to include the ZT3 Missile AT Systems)
- AC (Ratel 90) Squadron to 61 Mech
- AC (Ratel 90) Squadron to 4 SAI
- Tank (Olifant) Squadron to 4 SAI
- Tank (Olifant) Squadron to 61 Mech

Planning

The above forces, including their armour components, were committed piecemeal, often "too little too late", as the operations escalated. This gradual escalation can be attributed to changing threat perceptions of the opposing forces, political objectives, strategic and operational objectives, and typical "mission creep".

Implementation

At the start of these operations, the only armour involved in the conflict was the AC squadrons deployed to Sector 10, 32 Bn and 61 Mech, all stationed internally in Namibia. This was followed by 32 Bn deployed into Angola with their armour element (the only one with Ratel ZT3s). Later 61 Mech with their AC squadron deployed into Angola. Then 4 SAI with ACs and Olifant squadron, followed by 61 Mech, which also received an Olifant MBT squadron.

During Operation Hooper and Packer, a tank regiment was used with infantry support, albeit with only two squadrons. Eventually, by the time of Operation Packer and Excite, there was a tank regiment (minus one squadron). Initially, all the armour elements were used in the infantry support role and employed and integrated with their respective battalions.

Operational Use

The Olifant Mk1A played a significant role during the conventional phase of the South African Border War, during operations Moduler, Hooper, Packer, and Excite. Initially, 24 Olifant Mk1 and Mk1A tanks were deployed during the former three, with 13 tanks later participating in the latter operation in June 1988. The Olifant tanks, which were outnumbered six-to-one against T-54/55 tanks were tasked with countering the armoured forces of FAPLA.

The Olifant Mk1A made its combat debut with E-Squadron during Operation Moduler (August 1987 – January 1988). The engagement with FAPLA's 16th Brigade at Chambinga on 9 November 1987, marked a key moment, with Lieutenant Hein Fourie knocking out the first T-54/55 using an Olifant Mk1A tank. This was a notable achievement, as it was the first tank-to-tank kill for the Olifant Mk1A in Angola. The tank's first test under combat conditions proved successful, setting the stage for further operations.

Operation Hooper commenced on 2 January 1988, with F-Squadron from the School of Armour leading the charge. The Olifant Mk1A showcased its power on 3 January 1988, during this operation, where SADF tank crews employed HEAT rounds effectively against both armoured and soft-skinned vehicles. The preference for HEAT rounds arose from their ability to deliver a significant visual impact upon hitting targets, as well as their ability to engage entrenched tanks. The dense bush and limited visibility often restricted engagements, with tank battles typically occurring within ranges of 50–150m (55–154yd). The squadron successfully dislodged FAPLA's 21st Brigade from the Cuatir River, culminating in a seizure of the objective by January 13.

However, Operation Hooper saw its share of challenges. In the subsequent offensive on Tumpo 1 and Tumpo 2, a Cuban counterattack resulted in the damage of one Olifant Mk1A, and anti-tank mines immobilised two tanks from the Citizen Force Squadron. Despite efforts to recover the tanks, they were abandoned due to heavy enemy artillery and ground fire. This highlighted the brutal nature of the combat. Despite these losses, Cuban and FAPLA forces suffered significantly, with 21 T-54/55 tanks destroyed and approximately 480 casualties reported.

Operation Excite, which took place in June 1988, saw further deployments of the Olifant Mk1A tanks. The tanks participated in assaults on FAPLA positions, and further successes were achieved with several T-54/55s destroyed. During a minefield crossing, Regiment Molopo's Olifant Mk1A troop leader, Dean Kuhnert, described how his tank was severely jolted by a triple TM-57 anti-tank landmine, leaving it immobilised but still operational after an in-field repair.

Conclusion

The Olifant Mk1A emerged as a true African MBT, tailored to the Southern African battlespace's unique operational and tactical challenges. Through ingenuity and resourcefulness, the South African arms industry successfully upgraded the 40-year-old Centurion platform into an effective modern MBT, capable of going toe to toe with numerically superior enemy tanks. The Olifant Mk1A's performance in combat proved its effectiveness, particularly against Soviet-supplied T-54/55 and T-62 tanks.

Soon, however, the Olifant Mk1A would undergo a significant transformation with the introduction of the Mk1B a complete rebuild initiated by the South African defence industry. This upgrade aimed to enhance the Olifant's armour protection and mobility, making it an even more formidable opponent to the T-55 and T-62 tanks commonly encountered in the region. With these improvements, the Mk1B became an even greater threat on the battlefield, further cementing the Olifant's reputation as a capable and resilient MBT suited for the unique challenges of Southern Africa's military landscape.

Bibliography

Books

Abbot, P., Heitman, H.R. & Hannon, P., *Modern African Wars (3): South-West Africa*. (Oxford: Osprey Publishing, 1991)

Botha, W.C., de Vries, R., Ehlert, J, Haddad, W., Nell, J.T., Savides, T. & van der Westhuizen, A.J.O., *Ratel: The making of a Legend. Volume 2: Life with Ratel*. (Pretoria: BusinessPrint, 2020)

Camp, S. & Heitman, H.R., *Surviving the ride: A pictorial history of South African manufactured mine-protected vehicles* (Pinetown: 30° South Publishers. 2014)

de Vries, R., *Eye of the Firestorm: Strength lies in mobility* (Tyger Valley: Naledi, 2013)

de Vries, R., Burger, C. & Steenkamp, W. *Mobile Warfare for Africa: On the Successful Conduct of Wars in Africa and Beyond – Lessons Learned from the South African Border War* (Solihull: Helion and Company, 2018)

Harmse, K. & Sunstan, S., *South African Armour of the Border War 1975-89*. (Oxford: Osprey Publishing, 2017)

Heitman, H.R. *Krygstuig van Suid-Afrika*. (Struik Publihers, 1988)

Munro, B. *The Centurion tank*. (Ramsbury: The Crowood Press, 2005)

Steenkamp, W. & Heitman, H.R. *Mobility Conquers: The Story of 61 Mechanised Battalion Group 1978-2005* (Solihull: Helion & Company Limited, 2016)

Stiff, P. *Taming the Landmine* (Alberton, South Africa: Galago Publishing, 1986)

Van der Waag, I. *A military history of modern South Africa* (Jeppestown: Jonathan Ball Publishers, 2015)

Websites

ARMSCOR, (2024, January). Armscor reports Significant progress on G5 and G6 upgrades. https://www.armscor.co.za/wp-content/uploads/2024/01/Armscor-reports-significant-progress-on-G5-and-G6-upgrades.pdf

Army-Guide.Com, (2012). The G6 Still outgunning the competition. http://army-guide.com/eng/article/article_2406.html

DefenceWeb, (2009, January 20). SANDF projects: Past, present & future. https://www.defenceweb.co.za/sa-defence/sa-defence-sa-defence/sandf-projects-past-present-future/

DefenceWeb, (2011, June 29). Army cares for Casspir. https://www.defenceweb.co.za/land/land-land/army-cares-for-casspir/

DefenceWeb, (2011, December 13). Fact file: Denel FV2 Bateleur Multiple Launch Rocket System (MLRS). https://www.defenceweb.co.za/resources/fact-files/fact-file-denel-fv2-bateleur-multiple-launch-rocket-system-mlrs/?catid=79%3Afact-files&Itemid=159

DefenceWeb, (2011, April 18). Fact file: G6 L45 self-propelled towed gun-howitzer. http://www.defenceweb.co.za/index.php?option=com_content&view=article&id=13537:fact-file-g6-l45-self-propelled-towed-gun-howitzer-&catid=79:fact-files&Itemid=159

DefenceWeb. (2013, November 30). South African National Defence Force. http://www.defenceweb.co.za/index.php?option=com_content&view=article&id=29273:south-africa&catid=119:african-militaries&Itemid=255

DefenceWeb. (2019, November 20). Rheinmetall resets the range goal posts. https://www.defenceweb.co.za/featured/rheinmetall-resets-the-range-goal-posts/

Denel, (2012). The G6 Still outgunning the competition after 25 years. http://admin.denel.co.za/uploads/41_Denel_Insights.pdf

Dickens, P. (2019). I got him! I got him! I got him! https://samilhistory.com/2019/06/17/i-got-him-i-got-him-i-got-him/#comments

GlobalSecurity.org, (2015). Olifant Mk1B. https://www.globalsecurity.org/military/world/rsa/olifant-1b.htm

GlobalSecurity.org, (2016). Hoefyster (Horseshoe) / Badger. https://www.globalsecurity.org/military/world/rsa/badger.htm

GlobalSecurity.org, (2017). Wheel versus track. http://www.globalsecurity.org/military/systems/ground/wheel-vs-track.htm

NAMMO. (2018). NAMMO ammunition handbook (5th ed.). https://www.nammo.com/globalassets/pdfs/amm obook/nammo_ammo_handbook_aw_screen.pdf

National Defence Industry Council, (2017). Defence industry strategy: Version 5.8, draft. http://www.dod.mil.za/advert/ndic/doc/Defence%20Industry%20Strategy%20Draft_v5.8_Internet.pdf

Opticoel, (2022). Anti-Aircraft Automatic Sight ZAP 23. https://www.opticoel.com/products/anti-aircraft-automatic-sight-zap-23/

Ordnance & Munitions Forecast. (2015). G6 Renoster 155mm self-propelled howitzer. https://www.forecastinternational.com/archive/disp_pdf.cfm?DACH_RECNO=1105

SA Army, (2010), Weapon systems infantry: Grenade launchers, http://www.army.mil.za/equipment/weaponsystems/infantry/Y2_Y3_Grenade_Launchers.htm

SA Army, (2010). Weapon systems infantry: Machine guns, http://www.army.mil.za/equipment/weaponsystems/infantry/Machine_Guns.htm

SA-SOLDIER.COM. (2019). Buffel. https://www.sa-soldier.com/data/07-SADF-equipment/

Venter, D, (2023, June 3). Armoured Springbok. *Classic Military Vehicle*. Key Military. https://www.keymilitary.com/article/armoured-springbok

War in Angola, (2017). Vehicle specifications, 4:14. http://www.warinangola.com:8088/Default.aspx?tabid=1051

Washington Post, (1988, October 23). S. Africa unveils war machine for sale abroad. https://www.washingtonpost.com/archive/politics/1988/10/23/s-africa-unveils-war-machine-for-sale-abroad/47974c0b-101b-4d9b-9e54-c303061f3db2/

Facebook

Beyleveldt, J., (2017, September 16). *SA Pantserskool – SA Army School of Armour (SAW/SANW)* [Facebook post]. Facebook. https://www.facebook.com/groups/2609116067/posts/

Collins, D. C., (2017, September 16). *SA Pantserskool – SA Army School of Armour (SAW/SANW)* [Facebook post]. Facebook. https://www.facebook.com/groups/2609116067/posts/

Gardner, D., (2017, September 30). *Former Director OMC Engineering. SA Pantserskool – SA Army School of Armour (SAW/SANW)* [Facebook post]. Facebook. https://www.facebook.com/groups/2609116067/posts/

Jordan, L., (2017, September 16). *Tankers in Angola* [Facebook post]. Facebook. https://www.facebook.com/groups/435796636442928/posts/

Jordan, L., (2017, September 30). *Tankers in Angola* [Facebook post]. Facebook. https://www.facebook.com/groups/435796636442928/posts/

Naish, H., (2017, September 30). *Tankers in Angola* [Facebook post]. Facebook. https://www.facebook.com/groups/435796636442928/posts/

Sabatier, P., (2015, December 6). *This is not a front for something... it's a Casspir appreciation group* [Facebook post]. Facebook. https://www.facebook.com/groups/19835125223/posts/

Sabatier, P., (2015, December 6). *This is not a front for something... it's a Casspir appreciation group* [Facebook post]. Facebook. https://www.facebook.com/groups/19835125223/posts/10153130998320224/

Schafer, A., (2017, October 6). *SA Pantserskool – SA Army School of Armour (SAW/SANW)* [Facebook post]. Facebook. https://www.facebook.com/groups/2609116067/posts/

Uys, C., (2017, September 30). *Tankers in Angola* [Facebook post]. Facebook. https://www.facebook.com/groups/435796636442928/posts/

Interviews and Private Correspondence

Eland

Ansley, L., (2019, June 30). *Eland 20 armoured car* [Facebook post]. Pantserbond/Armour Association.

Bowden, N., (2019, June 12). *Cpt SANDF. Eland armoured car* [Facebook post]. Pantserbond/Armour Association.

Gardner, D., (2019, June 12). *Former Director OMC Engineering. Eland hull and turret development* [Facebook post]. Pantserbond/Armour Association.

Marais, S., (2019, June 14). *Eland armoured car* [Telephone message]. Pantserbond/Armour Association.

Savides, A., (2019, June 12). *Brig Gen (retd). Eland hull and turret development* [Facebook post]. Pantserbond/Armour Association.

Selfe, A., (2019, June 12). *Eland lights* [Facebook post]. Pantserbond/Armour Association.

Schenk, R., (2019, June 12). *SSgt (retd). Eland turret rear tube uses* [Facebook post]. Pantserbond/Armour Association.

Buffel

Barnard, C., (2019, October 20). *Buffel production at 61 Base Workshop* [Facebook post]. GRENSOORLOG/ BORDER WAR 1966–1989.

Beyl, M., (2019, October 22). *Operation Sceptic 1980* [Facebook post]. SMOKESHELL.

Bouwer, M., (2019, September 20). *Buffel operation doctrine* [Facebook post]. GRENSOORLOG/ BORDER WAR 1966–1989.

Haarhoff, J., (2019, November 12). *First line amm o* [Facebook post]. GRENSOORLOG/ BORDER WAR 1966–1989.

Hattingh, D., (2019, October 4). *Cover photo context* [Facebook post]. GRENSOORLOG/ BORDER WAR 1966–1989.

Joubert, K., (2019, October 23). *International sales of Buffels by ARMSCOR* [Facebook message].

Joubert, K., (2019, November 2). *Buffels history and technical details* [Email].

Myburgh, A., (2019, October 1). *Operation Sceptic 1980* [Facebook post].

Savides, A., (2019, October 4). *Brig Gen (retd) – 61 Base Workshop insights* [Facebook message].

Swanepoel, D., (2019, September 20). *Buffel operation doctrine* [Facebook post]. GRENSOORLOG/ BORDER WAR 1966–1989.

Van der Linde, S., (2019, September 20). *Buffel operation doctrine* [Facebook post]. GRENSOORLOG/ BORDER WAR 1966–1989.

Van der Merwe, C., (2019, October 4). *First 19 Buffels* [Facebook post]. GRENSOORLOG/ BORDER WAR 1966–1989.

Widd, P., (2019, September 20). *Buffel operation doctrine* [Facebook post]. GRENSOORLOG/ BORDER WAR 1966–1989.

Ratel

Savides, A. (2016, November 5). *Ratel development, history and application* [Facebook message].

G6

Du Rand, F., (2020, June 21). *G6-SPAAM project details* [WhatsApp message].

Heitman, H., (2020, June 21). *G6-SPAAM insights* [Facebook post]. South African Defence Industry & Military Related.

SANDF personnel., (2017, April 27). *G6-45 system [Vehicle inspection]*. School of Artillery, Klipdrift Military Base, Potchefstroom.

Potgieter, S., (2020, March 31). *G6 Rhino Self-Propelled Howitzer– Vehicle* [Facebook post]. South African Defence Industry & Military Related.

Van Heerden, A., (2020, June 20). *G6-SPAAM details* [WhatsApp message].

Bateleur

De Jager, A., (2018, November 11). *Bateleur FV2* [Facebook message].

De Villiers, D. J., (2018, December 3). *Bateleur platform background* [Email message].

Heyneke, D., (2018, November 16). *Bateleur FV2 project and Visarend training* [Facebook message].

SANDF personnel, (2017, April 25). *Bateleur FV2 [Vehicle inspection]*. School of Artillery, Klipdrift Military Base, Potchefstroom.

SANDF personnel, (2018, September 21). *Bateleur FV2 [Vehicle inspection]*. African Aerospace and Defence 2018, Waterkloof Air Force Base, Pretoria.

Olifant MK1A

Carroll, S., (2017, October 2). *Staff perspective – SA Armour Museum* [Email message].

Erasmus, R., (2017, October 2). *Chairman's commentary – SA Armour Museum* [Email message].

Retief, A., (2017, October 27). *GOC SA Army Armour Formation insights* [Message]. SA Armour Museum.

About the Author

Prof Dewald Venter is an accomplished academic, military historian, and published author with a distinctive focus on the psychological, cultural, and heritage dimensions of conflict. He holds a PhD in Tourism Management and is currently an Associate Professor at the Vaal University of Technology, where he specialises in travel motivation, life domains, quality of life.

Renowned for his research into military heritage, dark tourism, and adventure combat sports, Prof Venter has authored numerous peer-reviewed publications and conference presentations. His pioneering work explores the intersection of personal well-being, tourism, and military experience, particularly among veterans and re-enactors.

A recognised authority on armoured warfare history in Southern Africa, a frequent contributor to respected military publications such as *Classic Military Vehicle* and *Tank Encyclopaedia*, he has also served as a military vehicle consultant to several international gaming studios.

Prof Venter is an honorary council member of the SA Armour Museum and a frequent guest speaker on South African military vehicle history. His passion for preserving and interpreting South Africa's armoured legacy is evident in both his academic and public engagement work. Through his writing, he offers unique, experience-based insights into the realities of combat, *esprit de corps*, and the lived experiences of soldiers.